The Shorebased Officer

THE SHOREBASED SAILOR

What you need to know before you go to sea

John Myatt
BA, Cert Ed, Dip Ed Tech
Yachtmaster Instructor

HEINEMANN   KINGSWOOD

Heinemann Kingswood
Michelin House, 81 Fulham Road, London SW3 6RB

LONDON MELBOURNE
JOHANNESBURG AUCKLAND

First published 1988

ISBN 0 434 98125 7

Photoset & printed in Great Britain by
Redwood Burn Limited, Trowbridge, Wiltshire and
bound by Pegasus Bookbinding, Melksham, Wiltshire

To Neil and to Geoffrey (my most confident crew).

Acknowledgements

My grateful thanks to my son, Neil, and to my wife, Rosalind, for their invaluable help in preparing the manuscript.

Contents

Introduction

The need for *The Shorebased Sailor*

Knots

Safety of the Boat

Safety Equipment

Personal Safety

Skippering and Safety

Steering and Sailing Rules (Part B)

Lights and Shapes (Parts C and D)

Sound Signals

Charts

Tools of the Trade

Compasses

The Log

What are Tides?

Position fixing

Position estimation

Lights

Buoyage

Leading and Clearing Lines

Pilotage Planning

Position Fixing Devices

Radar

Weather

Tides
Charts and Publications

Victualling

Safety

List of illustrations, tables and diagrams

The author and publisher wish to thank the following for their assistance in providing illustrations:

Figs. 6.1, 6.2,   Admiralty Charts and Publications, by
7.4,   permission of The Hydrographer of the Navy
8.1, 8.2, 8.8,
9.1, 9.2, 9.3, 9.6, 9.7,
10.2,
A.6, A.7, A.8

Fig. 10.4   *Cruising Association Handbook*
                         (Cruising Association, 1981)

Figs. 7.2, 7.3   *The MacMillan & Silk Cut Nautical Alamanac*
                         (Macmillan, 1986 & 1988)

Thanks are also due to the London Yacht Centre and Upper Deck Chandlery (Fowey), for their advice and assistance.

Introduction

When I was planning this book, I picked up a volume on sailing and one *whole* chapter (parts of others too) was full of things like: 'Now feed the bolt rope into the luff groove' and, 'Next take up the tension on the outhaul', 'ease the topping lift and adjust the kicking strop' . . . and so it went on. Do you know what I am talking about? If you do, I bet you have learnt it *on a boat.* To learn this kind of technical detail from a book you would have to sit on the deck, with the book in one hand and dictionary in the other, while you did all the adjusting. Is this a realistic way of going about things? Can you learn practice through theory?

The need for *The Shorebased Sailor*

Should you learn the theory first or should you learn the practice?

Having taught a lot of people to sail, I think you have to do a bit of both. The way sailing training systems work in most countries means that courses are either one or the other. Practical course instructors will tell you: 'I have not got the time in five or six days to teach all the theory they need!' Shorebased courses are normally limited to about 40 hours of teaching time and instructors on these say: 'There is too much to teach. If only they knew something before they came on a course.'

There are problems with both types of course. That means that everyone trying to learn has a problem. I know, I teach both courses! This book is an attempt to help. It does not attempt to teach everything. For one thing I don't *know* everything! I have a book which says on its cover: 'All you need to know about sailing'. It's a lot thinner than this book too. What I have tried to do is take the things you can do at home, on your own, and explain them. When, after reading this book, you go on either a shorebased, or a practical, course, you should be a lot better off.

If you don't intend to take any theory courses, this book is also for you. You will still need the practice, but the book will help.

Sailing is a 'fun' activity. If you don't enjoy it, why do it? There seems to me to be no reason why the theory part has to be a chore and only the practice fun. This book is written with that in mind.

1

The Language of Sailing

What you will learn

The names of parts of the boat and also some terms that are used on boats to give directions. You will not learn the names of everything. We are concerned only with essentials.

By the time you have completed the chapter you will know

Enough terms to enable you to identify essential equipment and to understand many of the instructions given by a skipper to the crew.

What you will need

Either: access to a yacht ashore or afloat on a mooring or pictures of yachts showing both inside and outside views. Boat sales brochures or a sailing magazine with reviews of new yachts will do. You do not have to be able to get aboard the vessel although it would help.

Why go sailing?

Sailing, in fact every form of boating, is one of the fastest growing leisure activities in the world. Interest has been on the increase for some years but the biggest single boost, I think, has been given by the loss, by the New York Yacht Club, of the America's Cup and its subsequent victorious return to the USA by the San Diego Yacht Club.

This is particularly ironic, because the muscular heroes of the professional racing circus form only a tiny minority of sailors. Most of us cannot afford the millions of dollars it takes to own the kind of yacht they sail and of course many of us don't want to race; we get our enjoyment from the sailing itself. The vast majority of sailors are perfectly normal, ordinary people who just want to enjoy a sport which is both relaxing and demanding, involves both individual skill and team work and which can be enjoyed by everyone of whatever age.

See the sparkle of excitement in the eyes of a ten-year-old lad, as I have seen it, as he sails a 33-foot yacht neatly onto a mooring in a crowded harbour. Watch a 60-year-old hoisting a sail on the foredeck. Share the quiet satisfaction of the housewife who sees the harbour entrance dead ahead, exactly on the course she calculated 40 miles back. This is sailing.

What is the magic?

'You're a different person when you get on a boat', said the son of one of my clients, looking quizzically, even a little wistfully, at his father as they came aboard for their second trip with me.

'So are you!' commented my son, who happened to be with us, to me. I know just what they both meant. We two fathers were both more relaxed, more fun to be with.

Sailing is fun

Perhaps the physical act of getting away from land and thus one's worldly cares has something to do with it. Perhaps it is the calming effect of the sea, the sense of space and freedom. Whatever the answer, it is true; sailing is fun.

One important factor is the feeling that it is really up to you. Sailing a boat is quite unlike driving a car, or even riding a bike. You really feel much closer to fundamentals when it is the elements, directly, that move you on the vast mass of water that is the sea. And then there is something to do with anxiety, knowing that you can't pull in to the side and wait for a friendly AA man.

This, I suspect, is why you have picked up this book in the first place. You want to try sailing, maybe you have tried already, and are anxious that you do it properly. That *is* where this book comes in.

What to expect

I will not teach you to sail from a book. There is only one way to learn to sail. Get on a boat with someone who knows how to sail, and who will let *you* actually do more than just watch.

What I *will* do is to give you some understanding of the skills so that you are aware, when you do go on a cruising boat, both of what *needs* doing and of *how to do* quite a lot of it. You will begin to understand the language too. The rest you will have to learn on board, because that is the right place for learning it.

The language

Pick up a book on sailing and what do you find? It's the same thing that you find when you get on a boat, or go into a yacht club, or stand anywhere listening to a group of sailing people talking about sailing. As a non-sailor amongst sailors, you find that there is a whole new language of words, a barrier designed to keep out all who are not already in on the secrets. Or is it really that?

Part of the object of this book is to break down, or is it 'climb over', this barrier so that you too can understand the language.

The theory

The fact is that there is a great deal of *theory* involved in sailing. There are terms, methods and principles, as well as rules and conventions. If you are going to take part in serious sailing, on the sea, out of sight of land, there are lots of things you must know and understand. There are ways of doing things that are not just fussy. They are essential. The sea is no respecter of fools. If you don't get them right you may drown!

You need not be frightened by this for, once the mystery is taken away, most of the things are not difficult to learn. Much of what you need to know can be learned, without difficulty, ashore. Some of it is actually a great deal easier to learn ashore than afloat – it deals with the things you can learn without a boat.

Once you have learned the things in this book you can go on a boat with a pretty good idea of what is happening. You will know what most of the things you see around you are, and also how to find out *where* you are. You will, in fact, be quite a useful person to have aboard. You will still have a lot of practical things to learn and you will not need a book in your hand to learn them. The old sailors used to say: 'One hand for the ship and one for yourself'. What will happen if one of yours is holding a book?

Breaking the code

There is so much special language in sailing that to understand it is like breaking a code. I think there are several reasons for this. In the first place sailing has been around far, far longer than most other occupations. Even Neanderthal man, sitting astride his dead tree trunk to paddle across the river, must have had a special sort of grunt to mean: 'Don't paddle that way or this log will roll and feed us all to the crocodiles'. Only a special, unambiguous signal would have been quick enough to be effective. That is the nub of all the 'special' language.

Precision

Languages are *meant* for people who know them. Jargon is quicker, more precise, less open to wrong interpretation. Often the words are the same in several languages. Ask an Englishman, a Dutchman, a Belgian, Dane or Frenchman what a boom is and all will know the answer. If you are sitting in the cockpit of a yacht with an individual from each of these countries, and notice you are about to gybe, a shout of 'Boom!' will cause them all to duck which could be rather useful.

You will notice that I have underlined five words in the last paragraph. Each of these words is actually a jargon word from sailing. I suspect that most readers will understand them all, except perhaps for '*gybe*', but I wonder if you knew that they all had sailing connections?

The need to know

One of the problems, not exclusive to sailors, is that those who are in the know often do use their jargon to exclude outsiders. When this happens its usefulness as a clear, economical and precise way of expressing important things quickly, ceases. Remember this as you learn. The jargon word is at its most useful when everyone hearing it understands its precise meaning.

In this chapter I will introduce you to a number of new words which you will need in the following chapters. As well as these words, there are a great many more which name the parts of the boat, its equipment, actions one takes when sailing, etc. All this in the first chapter would be very daunting, so I have put a lot of it instead into Appendix B. The rest is spread through the text. All the important words which you may not know are explained in the Glossary.

Finding the right word

As I write I have tried to put each new word into its context so that, for the most part, you should be able to get the meaning from the text. I have also put new words in capital letters when they appear for the first time. If, when reading a chapter, you find a word you don't understand, then use the Glossary. This has the words listed in alphabetical order in the normal way. Only on the first occasion that a jargon word is introduced in the text is it written in capital letters. You may know the word or, by reading the text, be able to understand the meaning. If not, go to the Glossary section and look at the much fuller meaning given. You should do this because it will not be explained in the text when it occurs again.

Appendix B

Appendix B, as mentioned earlier, is also a collection of words, but it is different from a normal glossary. It is in a narrative form. It is intended to be used as a lesson to learn both the names of parts and other special terms. Just by reading it you may find that you can say: 'I know what that is now'. You could learn the terms by studying Appendix B in isolation, but try to avoid this if possible.

You will learn much more quickly by taking the book to a yacht and finding the things I shall mention. You do not have to be sailing for this. Go and stand on the pontoon of a marina, or visit a boat show. Find a friend who will let you wander over his boat. Failing all these, take a sailing magazine and study the pictures of all the boats you would like to own. This is quite an enjoyable exercise.

Parts of the boat

Figure 1.1 is a diagram of a sailing boat. It has two triangular sails hung on one mast. The sails have points at the top and are broad based. The figure shows a sloop rigged boat. The last sentence says the same thing as all the first three together. This sort of economy of words is very useful and will help you right from the first time you sail.

If you can confidently name all the parts indicated by letters in Figure 1.1, you may not need Appendix B, or perhaps a brief look at it may be enough. The answers are in Appendix A in case you are not totally sure. If you can't name them all, I suggest you take the slower route: study Appendix B in the way I have suggested, and stay with me.

Directions

In sailing, all direction terms are related to the boat. Often you can not see anything else! Towards the front of the vessel is FORWARD and towards the back is AFT. Things that are behind your boat are ASTERN and things in front of it are AHEAD. The widest part of the vessel is the BEAM so that things off to the side are usually related to the beam.

ON THE BEAM is normally something more or less at right angles to the direction in which the vessel points. Otherwise it is either forward of the beam or ABAFT the beam. Since the back corners are called QUARTERS, anything that is far enough abaft the beam to be in that direction is said to be ON THE QUARTER.

The sides of the boat are either PORT, which is the left side when facing towards the front (or FORWARD), or STARBOARD which is the right side when facing forward. The word FINE is sometimes used

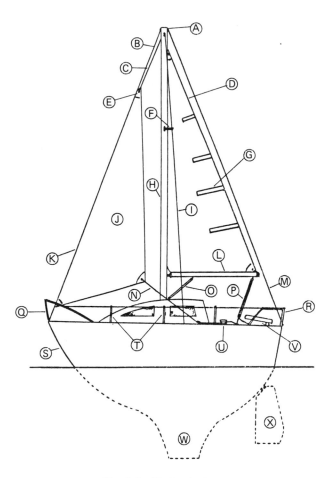

Fig. 1.1 Parts of a boat

to indicate near to, as in the expression 'cutting it fine'. Thus, 'fine on the port bow', means just to port of straight ahead.

The port side used to be called 'larboard' but the term is seldom heard now. The change of name probably came about as a result of the homeward-bound sailor in the English Channel talking of the larboard side as the port side, since it would literally be the side on which his home port lay. This name, in shouted orders, would be much easier to distinguish from starboard than the older name.

Figure 1.2 shows all the directions just mentioned in relation to the boat.

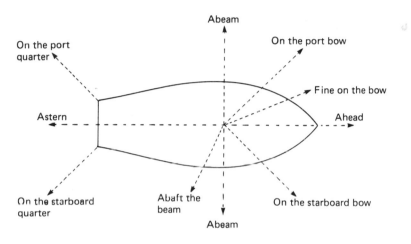

Fig. 1.2   Directions as seen from a vessel

That is the end of learning words for the moment. From now on you will find all the new words you need sprinkled in the text and explained as we go along.

In the next chapter you will learn the knots you will need to use on a sailing boat and something about ropes in general. You will be asked to *do things*. This will happen all the way through the book. If you do them as I suggest, you will get a lot more out of it. Before you start studying Chapter 2, you will need at least a few pieces of string; rope would be better still.

2

Ropes and Knots

What you will learn

Enough about the kinds of rope that are available to:
a) Know which is the best kind for a particular purpose.
b) Know how to look after your ropes.
   How to tie the seven basic knots and what to use them for.
   The uses and misuses of splices and how joins are made, also how to stop an end from fraying.

By the time you have completed the chapter you will know

All the knots that you will need on a sailing boat as well as how and when to use them.
   How to make a common whipping.
   Enough about ropes and their uses to make you a useful crew member.

What you will need

Ideally: Three pieces of rope about one metre long each. Two should be about 1 cm thick and the other about half that size. If the first two are different colours it will help.
   Some odd short bits of rope and some thin string to practise whipping. If you cannot get hold of some odd rope ends, then use thick string. Most chandlers will sell you odd short lengths of rope at very little cost, or you can use old pieces such as you can find on a beach.

Ropes

Not so very long ago, when ropes were made from natural fibres, it was usual to devote whole chapters to their properties and care. Now that ropes are mostly made from man-made materials so that they do not rot, this no longer seems to be the case. It is a pity, because modern ropes still need looking after if they are to serve you well. Although rope work is a practical subject, a little thought ashore, to gain some understanding of how ropes are made, used and looked after will help make *your* ropes last a lot longer.

Fitness for purpose

It was realised quite early that two types of rope were needed: those that would stretch easily, and those that would not. This is because ropes are needed for two different types of job. If you want to lift a weight with a block and tackle, the rope you use must have as little stretch as possible. Otherwise you will do an awful lot of work on the rope before anything happens to the weight! If one boat is towing another in a rough sea, the rope joining them will need to have lots of stretch to allow for the constant changes in pull as the two boats bob about. If it does not, the jerking of the rope will break it or damage the boats.

This thinking applies to all ropes used on boats. The other things that matter are concerned with strength, handling and wear. Will it be strong enough for the purpose? Is it easy to hold? Is it slippery or rough? Will it take a knot or splice? Will it rub through quickly or crack in use? Will it rot? Summed up, these questions ask whether the rope will do the job required for long enough. The answer depends on the material it is made of.

Materials

Ropes used for hoisting things, halliards for example, must be comfortable to pull and easy to secure, as well as being largely stretch free. You will often find that halliards are made of a combination of rope and wire. The former satisfies the first two properties, whilst the latter has hardly any stretch. Figure 2.1 shows some of the fibres in common use, together with their general properties.

Properties

With the quality of man-made fibres improving, you will find halliards of pre-stretched *Polyester* or of *Kevlar* on some boats. Nylon is uncomfortable to work with but has good strength and stretch properties so tends to be used for warps to tie the boat up. Polyester (Terylene) is more common for sheets, being kinder than nylon to hands.

Material	Properties					
	Strength	Resistance to Wear	Elasticity	Handling	Buoyancy	Cost
Polyester (Terylene)	Good	Good	Low	Comfortable	Sinks	Average
Nylon	Good	Good	High	Feels hard	Sinks	Average
Polypropylene	Fair	Fair	Low	Hard & slippery	Floats	Cheap
Kevlar	V. Good	Chafes	V. Low	Stiff, knots will slip	Sinks	High
Polythene	Poor	Poor	Low but becomes plastic	Rough, knots will jam	Nearly neutral	Cheap

Fig. 2.1   Properties of synthetic rope fibres

Notes:
1. All synthetic fibres have a greater resistance to rot than do natural fibres.
2. Braided ropes are usually stronger than laid ropes and are softer to handle.
3. Plaited rope is better for warps and anchor cable. It tangles less and has more give to it.

Polypropylene is very cheap but can hardly be considered as a yachtsman's rope. It is very easily damaged by chafe and quickly becomes brittle.

Causes of weakness

Modern ropes are largely rot free, but rot is not the only damage that they can suffer. Man-made fibres are often changed chemically by sunlight and can then become brittle. Salt crystals, and also particles of grit or sand which can collect between the fibres, can cut into them and weaken the rope without showing any visible signs of damage.

Although man-made fibres won't rot, they will melt. This can be a useful property if you want to seal the end of a rope or cut it with a hot knife, but it can be a disaster if friction or closeness to a high temperature causes the rope to heat up. Some fibres will soften in boiling water! Some will dissolve in a variety of chemicals, particularly oil-based ones.

Care of ropes

Abrasion and friction can be avoided by keeping ropes clean in use, and by checking pulley sheaves for freedom of movement. If a rope is to be passed over a rough – or even slightly rough – surface, it should be protected. A few short lengths of plastic hose to slide over your mooring lines where they run through a FAIRLEAD or onto a harbour wall, will increase their life tremendously.

Regular washing to remove salt and chemical contamination is well worthwhile. You can use one of the patent cleansers if you like, or a strong solution of washing-up liquid. Don't use things containing bleach or abrasives – even washing powders sometimes have these.

Coiling ropes

Always take the trouble to coil ropes for stowing or storage. A rope that is properly coiled and fastened will be less likely to tangle. This will mean it will be ready if you need to use it quickly. Learn to coil properly so that you avoid kinks. On LAID ropes, which are the ones that have three twisted strands, open the lays slightly as you coil them. This makes them hang better and they are much less likely to tangle or kink when re-used.

With BRAIDED ropes it does not matter so much, unless they have a laid core. Braided ropes are the ones that seem to have a coarsely-woven sheath over a core. The core may be braided or laid. If it is laid, you can tell by giving a twist in each direction before you start coiling. A laid core will make the rope feel harder when it is twisted with the lay. If so, treat it like laid rope and make a slight twist against the lay as you coil.

Plaited ropes, which will have four or more twisted parts, do not tangle easily and, although it looks messy, are actually best coiled in a series of figure eights, the very thing you are trying to avoid with laid rope. Plaited ropes are often used for anchors and for mooring lines.

Avoiding kinks

When using a laid rope for the first time you can reduce the chances of it kinking by pre-stretching it. To do this you have to uncoil the whole length and put tension on it. On re-coiling it, you will have to remove the twists that you now find in it.

As you coil a rope, always work any twists or kinks you find towards the free end. This means that if you are coiling the spare part of a rope that is in use, such as a halliard, you must start coiling from the attached end towards the free end.

Knots

To use a rope it has to be attached to something. There are two ways of doing this: with knots and with splices. It is not often appreciated that a knot weakens the rope. If a rope breaks it will normally break at a knot, unless it is badly worn elsewhere. The reason for this is that the fibres are bent more sharply in the knot than anywhere else, and so are more stressed. Some knots are better in this respect than others.

To describe a knot, the two ends are distinguished as THE STANDING PART, which is the bit that goes away and has, or will have, the tension on it, and the FREE END, that is the end that will remain loose.

As well as being concerned about the strength of the knot, the ease of tying and untying it are as important as is its reliability in use. A knot that comes undone *only when you want it to* is the right knot to use. In the old days of square riggers, as I have said before, the motto was: 'One hand for the ship and one for yourself'. All the commonly used knots aloft can be untied or 'broken' with one hand. Most can be tied with one hand too.

What knots

Pick up a book on knotting and you will find it is enough to frighten anyone who is just starting to learn. The way to approach the problem is to start with *uses*. The reason for tying a knot is that you want to *use* it. The Royal Yachting Association (RYA) syllabus only lists seven knots because, with these seven, you will have a knot for any job you need.

You will need to be able to make a temporary loop in the end of a rope, join two ropes together (perhaps of different sizes), tie in a REEF and stop the end of a rope running out of a block. You will also need to be able to attach a rope to something solid. It may be a bar, a ring or a BOLLARD, or perhaps a cleat. The following set of knots will do all these things. Figure 2.2 shows how to tie them.

Bowline

To make a loop in the end of a rope, a bowline is best. It weakens the rope less than most other knots and is easy to undo, even after it has got wet and been under great tension. All you have to do to break it, is turn the knot over and bend it so that the loop, which passes over the standing part and the free end, rolls away to loosen it. You cannot do this whilst it is under tension. In Figure 2.2 the bowline is drawn part-tied, as well as complete. Be sure that you get the loop in the standing part the right way up before you start weaving in the free end.

This is the knot used for attaching the sheets to the jib or for making a temporary loop to drop over a bollard. One bowline tied through another makes a secure but rather bulky way of joining two ropes together. Joining ropes with bowlines is a method that does allow chafe, however, so should only be used as a short-term measure.

Sheet bend

Use a sheet bend or double sheet bend to join two ropes of different sizes, such as attaching a light HEAVING LINE to a towing cable. It is a quick and secure knot provided it stays under tension. It is also quick to undo which can be useful when a heaving line is used to pass a tow. Do not use it as a long-term knot, such as for extending mooring lines. It is less secure when both ropes are of the same size.

If the ropes are *very* different in size a double sheet bend is used. In this, the thinner line is taken twice round the bend. To break either type, release the tension on the thinner line and pull the thicker end away from its standing part to open the bend. The thin line can then be slid off.

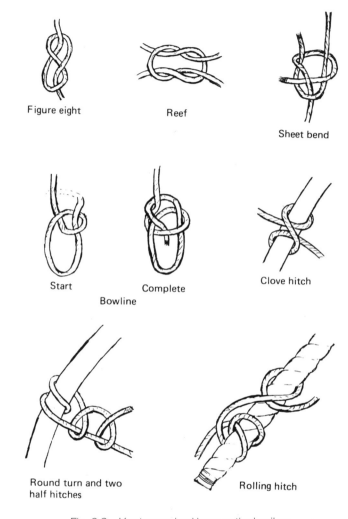

Fig. 2.2   Knots required by practical sailors

Reef knot

Sometimes called a square knot, the reef knot is used mainly for securing reefing ties or lashings. It depends for its strength on tension remaining on, and being equal in, both directions. To break the knot is easy. Either free end is brought from the side on which it leaves the knot, towards the opposite side, and is pulled sharply. This part of the rope is thus straightened and the other part can be slid off it.

Figure-of-Eight

This knot is sometimes called a stopper knot. It is used to make a stopper in the free end of a rope such as a sheet or halliard so that it will not run out through a sheave when let go. Unlike the overhand knot, it is easy to undo even when wet. Just take the loop which is round the standing part and roll it away from the bulk of the knot, and it will become loose.

Clove hitch

This is a temporary knot. It can be used to secure to a post or can be dropped over a bollard. Used in this way it reduces the strength of the rope very little, but is difficult to undo under tension. If there is low friction between the rope and the fixture it can work undone. The most common use of the clove hitch is to secure FENDERS which are hung over the sides of the boat to protect it when going alongside a jetty or pontoon. This is because it is quick to adjust and easy to remove. Just pull on the over-running loop and it comes free. Once finally set, a half hitch on the standing part will reduce the risk of the knot working loose.

Rolling hitch

This is a version of the clove hitch in which the first half hitch is made into a complete round turn. When the pull is on the end having the round turn, a great deal of friction is created and it can be tied on a straight and quite thick rope under tension, where it will hold without slipping. It is useful for taking the strain whilst removing a riding turn from a winch. It is broken in the same manner as a clove hitch.

Round-turn-and-two-half-hitches

This is the knot to use when securing a shore line to a ring or bar. It has good strength, is easy to undo under tension and is not subject to chafe. If the first half hitch is taken through the round turn it becomes a fisherman's or anchor hitch. This version is virtually impossible to undo when under tension and so is ideal for securing to the anchor ring.

Practice

The time to learn to tie these knots is ashore. Get yourself three short lengths (about 1 m each) of rope, two of the same diameter (about 10 mm) but of different colours. The third should be about half that thickness. You will find it easier, with ropes of different colours, to see how the knot is formed. Practise until you can tie them without looking. Use a chair for the solid bits. When you can tie them all with confidence you will be a very welcome crew member.

Splicing and whipping

Sometimes you need to make a permanent loop in the end of a rope, or a permanent join between two ropes. When you do, a splice should be used. A splice is neater, takes less rope and is much stronger than a knot, if well done.

I find that in practice there are very few occasions when I want a permanent eye splice. I do not like them in mooring ropes because they have an annoying habit of catching on anything, in sight or out of it, just at the crucial moment. Nothing is more disconcerting, or potentially dangerous, than becoming secured accidentally when you expect to be free. I once saw a demonstration of seamanship which came disastrously unstuck, or perhaps it should be stuck, from this cause.

The crew were all uniformed with navy jumpers, white trousers, the lot. All the crew were on board. Skipper, in blue blazer and white peaked cap, called: 'Let go springs!' It was duly done and the lines neatly retrieved. 'Let go bow!' The bow line was let go by the foredeck crew, a girl of about fifteen, who immediately started to bring it in.

'Let go aft!' called the skipper. He glanced round to see the small lad on the stern drop one end of the doubled rope over and start to pull in. Turning forward again, he put the engine in gear with enough revs to turn into the tide. On the port quarter the lad was pulling in the rope as fast as he could go and dropping it at his feet. The inevitable happened. As the end arrived at the shore cleat, the spliced eye in it neatly flipped itself onto the cleat and made fast.

Skipper was concentrating on his manoeuvre; the boat was now gathering way and the resulting jerk caused the lad to let go the rope which snaked out over the side as the boat began to move faster. The inboard end was still secured. The lad called out a warning that was not heard above the engine noise. When all the rope had run out it continued to stretch for a while.

The skipper then experienced a rapid deceleration that nearly shook him off his feet. The foredeck crew was now lying on her back. Skipper glanced astern and whipped the engine control into neutral. He said something – I don't know what. (I've led a very sheltered life!) The rope rapidly returned to its original length as the boat swung round with a crash into the one next-door.

Surprisingly, no real damage was done, except to pride. Skipper blamed first the lad, who was now in tears, before rounding on the foredeck crew. She would not be brow-beaten and gave him her opinion. Skipper's wife, who had taken no part in the proceedings, was called to account next. She took one look at the audience ashore and retreated back below.

This was a potentially tragic situation which caused a great deal of merriment ashore. Lessons should have been learned.

Spliced eyes

I only put spliced eyes in ropes if the loop is going to be in use for long periods. This could be a pick-up line from a mooring buoy or the end of a halliard that will be attached with a SHACKLE. In this case the loop should be protected from chafe by the use of a THIMBLE. This is a metal or hard plastic collar which fits tightly inside the loop and takes the strain. When the loop is to be a large one, perhaps to be slipped over a cleat, it is best protected by slipping on a length of soft plastic tubing before making the splice, so that the entire loop is protected.

A well executed eye splice, with the correct size thimble, can be virtually as strong as the original rope. If you learn to splice ashore and you practise on odd ends of rope, you will be able to do one if you need to, on board. Modern man-made fibre ropes are much stronger than the older natural fibre types, size for size. Because of this, you can normally repair a broken eye with a knot instead of a splice as a temporary measure.

Joining ropes by splicing is seldom needed now. With modern fibres, rope can be continuously spun to any length. End-to-end splices, however well done, do increase the thickness of the rope and this can cause problems with modern blocks. Similarly, back or end splices are best replaced with heat sealing and then whipping, on synthetic ropes.

Common whipping (shown in Figure 2.3) should be learned and practised. Follow the stages through, making sure that each successive turn is pulled tight and is set close to the previous one. Once you have covered a length of the rope of about twice its diameter, pass the free end through the loop formed at the start and pull both ends to tighten. Now pull on the end forming the loop until it disappears under the whipping. Both ends should be cut short. The end of the rope is cut off about half a diameter from the whipping and, on synthetic rope, heat sealed with a hot knife to finish.

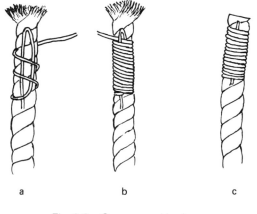

Fig. 2.3   Common whipping

Wire-to-rope joins

There are two forms of end-to-end splice that are still in common use. One is the joining of a rope tail to a wire halliard so that it can be pulled by hand. Such joins are difficult to do well and, since they are subject to great strains, are best left to the professionals. The use of pre-stretched Terylene or Kevlar halliards will avoid the need for wire-to-rope joins.

The other is the joining of an anchor warp to the anchor chain. This is not difficult to learn but I would only use it if the anchor is to be worked using a winch. The fibres on the inside of the rope are touching the chain and are thus subject to abrasion. However smooth the chain, sand can get in. This to me is a potential weakness which I would rather do without. I shackle my chain to the rope using a spliced eye with an oversize thimble. It is bulky, but safer.

In summary, as a newcomer to sailing, make sure that you can tie all the knots discussed. They are the *essential* ones. Common whipping I also consider as essential. Learning to splice can be very satisfying and is a useful, but not an essential, skill.

3

Anchors, Anchoring and Mooring

───────────── ⚓ ─────────────

What you will learn

Something of the history of anchors and how they have developed.
   The types of anchor in common use and their properties.
   How to decide the length of chain or rope to use.
   How to make your anchor work better.
   The things to consider when you choose an anchorage.
   What sizes of anchor and chain you will need.
   A little about moorings.

By the time you have completed the chapter you will know

Enough about anchors and anchoring to be able to make sensible choices about how and where to anchor and to assess the probable reliability of your anchoring.

What you will need

No special equipment is needed to study this chapter but you should try to examine some anchors, chain and cables in a chandler's so that you can get an idea of what the sizes and weights talked about mean.

If you want to leave your boat, go away and come back *and* find it where you left it, it has to be attached to something solid! The solid object must itself be sufficiently linked to the world so that it stays where it is.

In practice that means that your boat must be joined to land in some way, even if the only bit of land near you is some distance below both you and the surface of the water. You can't very easily bang a spike into the seabed, so an anchor is used. Its job is to create enough friction to keep it in position even when a gale of wind is trying, at the surface, to move your boat away.

Anchors historically

Anchors have been used as long as boats. In all regions of the world where boat remains have been found, the remains of anchoring devices have also been found. To start with they were often large oval stones with a groove cut right round them to hold a line. Sometimes a hole had been cut right through the stone which, presumably, made the connection more reliable.

As soon as man was able to fashion iron, he found that it worked better than stones. It is denser for a start. It can also be worked into shapes which will either dig into, or catch onto, the sea bed. This improved the reliability a great deal. Later he found that chain rather than rope, at least at the anchor end, worked even better.

Evolution

I have looked a little at the history because I think that modern sophistication has made a lot of people overlook the fundamentals of anchors. Their prime job is to make a reliable link with the sea bed. Since the anchor had to be carried in the same boat for which it was to be used, there was a great incentive to get the weight and size down without losing the basic performance.

For a long time two types were used. This was because it was soon found that no one design worked well in all situations. The two routes were a hook with a long narrow spike which stood a good chance of catching on rock or in weed, and a broader spade-shaped spike which did not work so well on rock or weed but which would give a better grip in sand or mud.

The next stage was the introduction of double-ended hooks, and then a bar fitted at right angles to the shaft on which the hooks were mounted. Both these ideas were intended to increase the chances of the hooks digging in. It was such a successful development that this particular design has remained in use, largely unchanged, to this day.

The traditional one with the rather narrow flukes has become the familiar FISHERMAN'S ANCHOR (Figure 3.1), still used today by fishermen who usually *need* to anchor on rock or weed. The broader-bladed version is the one seen on old warships, often fashioned mainly from oak banded with iron and with iron spade flukes. Using wood helped to keep the weight down whilst still allowing the larger size.

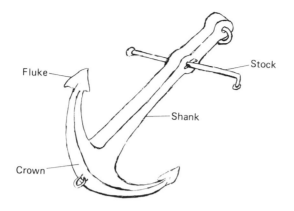

Fig. 3.1   Fisherman's anchor

Modern anchors

If you keep in mind the developments outlined, you should be able to see that all the modern types of anchor are related to these two original designs. Figure 3.2 shows the types you are likely to come across on pleasure boats and even large vessels. On yachts you will usually find the CQR (plough) anchor (standing for Chatham Quick Release) or DANFORTH which, since it stows flat, can be stored rather more easily.

Kedge anchor

The BRUCE ANCHOR is gaining in popularity and is a departure from the old ideas. It still does the same job but is made from one single piece of metal with no moving parts. This makes it very strong and less metal is needed for the same grip. It is an ideal anchor for a KEDGE. This is the anchor you row out with you in a small boat when you run aground, in order to help pull yourself off. Being lighter, it is easier to handle in a dinghy.

A kedge anchor should always be used on rope with only just enough chain to set it properly. This is because using all chain would make it too difficult to handle in a dinghy. To lay out a kedge, the end of the cable is attached to the boat, the anchor and all remaining cable being placed in the dinghy which is then rowed out, the cable being payed out from the dinghy as it goes.

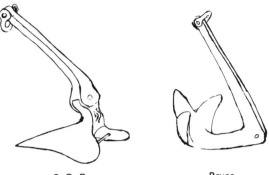

C. Q. R.   Bruce

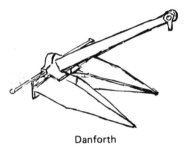

Danforth

Fig. 3.2   Anchors

Relative properties

Figure 3.3 gives an idea of the relative holding powers of different anchors in different substances. You will notice that, *still*, no one anchor does a perfect job under all conditions. Invent one, and you will make your fortune! Until then it is best to carry two types.

Which anchors?

In carrying two anchors I would settle for a CQR or Bruce as main anchor on a yacht, with the other as spare, possibly with a Fisherman's as a second spare. This would depend on how often I expected to be anchoring in weed or on rock. Neither the CQR, the Bruce nor the Fisherman's, of a size large enough to be useful, is easy to stow. I consider it anti-social to keep your main anchor hanging over the bow, but on some yachts it has to be done, no provision being made for it elsewhere.

Yacht Size	Anchor Weights (Kgs)				Cable Sizes (mm)	
	Fisherman	CQR	Danforth	Bruce	Chain	Rope
under 5m	20	10	10	7.5	6.5	12
5 – 8m	25	15	12	10	6.5	14
9 – 12m	30	17.5	15	15	8	16

Holding Properties of Each Type

Type of Bottom

	Fisherman	CQR	Danforth	Bruce
Mud	Fair	Good	Good	V. Good
Sand	Fair	Good	Good	V. Good
Shingle	Good	Good	Good	Good
Kelp	Good	Fair	Poor	Fair
Rock	V. Good	Fair	Poor	Fair
Power/weight ratio	Poor	Good	Good	Good

Fig. 3.3 Anchor types and properties

People often refer to the second anchor as the Kedge and carry a much lighter one than for the main anchor. It depends to some extent on the sailing you expect to do. I do think, if my main anchor breaks or fails to hold in a gale, that a much smaller spare may well not help very much.

Anchor cable

The anchor has to be made fast to the boat to be any use. The way it is linked is very important. The BITTER END is the end left in the boat when the anchor is out. This end must be attached permanently to the boat so that if the whole chain runs out, it is not lost. It must be attached in a way that is easy to release in an emergency. A piece of line that can be cut is best.

All anchors must have some chain attached, at least five metres for a boat up to about ten metres long. This is because the anchor only works if the pull on it is in a direction along the sea bed. Pull it even a little upwards and it will break out and lose its holding power. Chain also produces greater friction than rope in contact with the bottom, as well as being far less susceptible to wear.

The length of rope, chain or whatever between the boat and anchor is called the CABLE and it lies in the water in a curve, called the CATENARY. If it is all chain, because the metal is heavy, the cable retains its curve even when under tension. Provided the cable is long enough, the bottom part of the curve will be along the sea bed and the anchor will receive its pull in the right direction.

If a rope is used all the way to the anchor, since rope has very little weight in water, it can pull almost straight when under tension. This would break out the anchor. A short length of chain at the anchor end will improve the catenary shape so that the pull is still along the bottom.

Cable length

Even with some chain the SCOPE (the length needed from the surface to the anchor), when rope is used, must be much greater. As a guide, the *minimum* safe length with all chain, is three times the *maximum* depth of water. If a mixture of rope and chain is used, the *minimum* length should be increased to five times the maximum depth. If the bottom is not good HOLDING GROUND, perhaps shells, loose sand and so on, then the length should be increased still further. This should also be done in strong winds.

Swinging circle

If you put an anchor down where there is a strong tide, the boat will move round with the tide in a circle called the swinging circle. The size of this circle often causes confusion. Its precise size will depend on many things like the strength of the stream and the nature of the bottom.

It will never be as great as the length of cable, unless you have used far too little scope! It will be at its largest when using rope on a falling tide and when the tidal range is great. The maximum circle will have a radius something under 80 per cent of the scope with rope, and under 50 per cent with all chain. If you are using rope and other boats anchored near you are on chain, you must be careful that you do not swing into them when the tide turns. It is as well to check for this anyway. You can never be sure how much scope anyone else is using.

Choosing the spot

How do you know where to anchor? This will often be indicated on charts and in pilot books, which we shall look at in Chapters 6 and 10. In general you must not anchor anywhere where it may cause danger to yourself or others, or inconvenience to anyone. The bottom must be good holding ground and you must have enough water to float well clear of the bottom, even at low tide. How to check this point is covered in Chapter 7.

Marking the spot

A TRIPPING LINE is a light line attached to a small float and to the ring at the CROWN of the anchor (see Figure 3.1). It does two jobs. If you make the length of line about the same as the maximum depth of water, it means that it will mark the position of your anchor. If the anchor gets caught on some obstruction on the sea bed, by pulling on the tripping line, you can often turn the anchor upside down, or CAPSIZE it, and so get it free.

Marking the position of your anchor can be a mixed blessing. The idea is to be able to see, and let others see, where it is. In practice, in my experience, it will be run over, caught on someone's propeller or, as I had on one occasion, be picked up by someone else to use as a mooring!

You can bring the tripping line on board, tying it at intervals to the anchor cable with light line. In this way it is safe and yet can be used if your anchor gets caught. I only ever use one when I know the bottom is likely to be FOUL.

Reliability

Great arguments rumble on about which is better, rope or chain. I will try to give you all the pros and cons and let you enter the controversy on a basis of some knowledge!

Chain is stronger, size for size, although heavier; it generates more friction, produces a better catenary shape and is very unlikely to wear through in use. It also rusts, produces shock, snatch loads at the anchor in rough water and can break suddenly with no obvious visible defect.

Rope is light so that you can carry more and thicker without a weight problem; it is elastic and so does not generate shock loads at the anchor, (modern rope) is virtually rot free and has very reliable strength properties. It also wears easily if run over a rough object, can be cut by the propeller of a passing vessel and has a much less efficient catenary shape.

A well-documented account of a number of vessels storm bound in a bay claimed that all the yachts lying to chain only dragged their anchors, whilst all those lying to rope held throughout the storm. The argument put forward was that the snatch loads in the very violent seas caused the anchors on chain to break out. We are not told, however, either what type of anchor each boat was using, or their respective weights.

Improving the holding

Various ways of improving the holding ability of an anchor are available. Two anchors may be VEERED (or put out) either on the same, or separate cables. If both are of about the same weight, on the same cable, the holding power is about three or four times that of one anchor alone. Figure 3.4 illustrates both methods.

If two cables are used, the anchors must be separated so that the pull is at an angle of not more than about 30 degrees between them. If they are too close, they may come together and foul each other. It is essential that the two cables are of the same or very similar size if they are to be really effective. One of chain and one of rope is not much good. Modern boats, with relatively short, deep, fin keels tend to veer back and forth when at anchor in strong winds, and so the tension keeps switching from one cable to the other, rather than being shared between them.

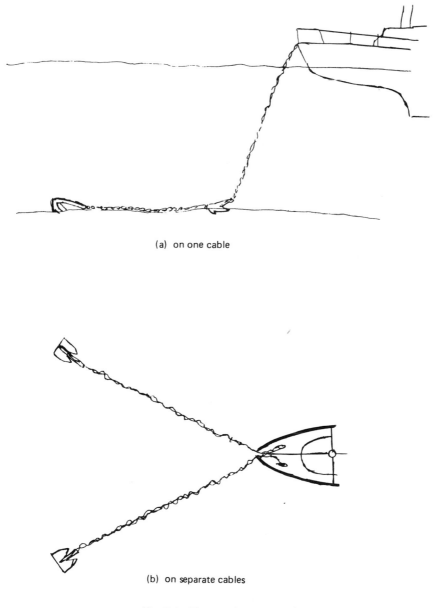

(a) on one cable

(b) on separate cables

Fig. 3.4 Two anchors veered

Moorings

The techniques for picking up or letting go a mooring are best taught in practice. A couple of points about moorings need to be said, however. First, a mooring is exactly the same thing as an anchor whilst you are attached to it. It does the same job and the same rules apply. The difference between them is that when you leave an anchorage, you detach your vessel from the sea bed and take the whole mooring with you; when you leave a mooring, you detach the vessel from the top of the chain, leaving anchor and chain behind.

This brings me to the second point. The mooring is attached or anchored to the sea bed. This may be done with one or several anchors, or it may be done with a large weight. However it is done you will not be able to look at the condition of either chain, weight or any of the fastenings very often. This means that they must be much more substantial than you will need to use for your anchor chain. Weight does not matter here, so long as the top end has an adequate float to prevent it sinking when you let go. In any event you must have your whole mooring tackle checked regularly, once a year at least. The boat will be hanging on it for a large part of its life and you won't always be there to see if it breaks!

Most people like to have chain right on to the boat on a mooring, for added security. This practice is understandable but it does mean that the tackle is subject to shock loads, as are the deck fittings. A good compromise is to have a thick nylon rope strop, properly spliced and thimbled, connected to the main mooring chain. This can be brought aboard and secured to a cleat, remembering to protect from chafe. A chain strop is then also connected to the main chain and brought on board to a separate cleat. The chain strop should be a little longer than the rope one. On a snatch load the rope will give a little and so, act as a shock absorber. If it, or the deck fitting breaks, the chain will save you losing the boat.

The chain strop will swing a good deal and will both wear and corrode much faster than the rest of the chain. It needs to be checked regularly, and replaced when it shows signs of wear.

It is worth remembering that shackles tend to corrode faster than chain, they also need checking regularly. You will, of course, have the pins SEIZED (tied with wire), so that they cannot work loose.

Every year in our harbour some boats break loose. The reason is always the same, neglected ground tackle. Be warned, chain is expensive but boats are a lot more so. The old saying that a chain is as strong as its weakest link is a statement of fact. Adequate strength cable in good condition does wonders for your peace of mind. Proper mooring and anchoring are vital parts of yacht safety, which is the subject of the next chapter.

4

Safety at Sea

What you will learn

What the likely causes are of risks to safety of a boat and of its crew, and how to avoid or to reduce these risks.

What you can do in the event of a hole being made in your boat and how to plan your response to damage.

The safety equipment that should be carried and how to use it.

How to keep yourself and others safe.

What you need to do if someone falls overboard.

How to be a safety conscious skipper.

By the time you have completed the chapter you will know

The kinds of things that can go wrong on a boat and how you can avoid or reduce the effects.

How to deal with problems involving safety.

How to call for assistance.

How to plan for safety.

What you will need

No special equipment is needed to study this chapter but you should try to examine the items of safety equipment mentioned, particularly flares and safety harness so that you know how to use them *before* you need them.

If you can get onto a yacht, particularly if you are intending to charter or buy it, have the book with you and try to imagine how you would deal with the situations described in this chapter.

No one needs to be afraid of the sea. Yet everyone who goes on, into, under or even near the sea needs to have respect for it. The key is respect, not fear.

You have to take sensible precautions. You have to be aware of the huge power of the sea; a power that can show itself quite quickly. So long as you do these things, you can enjoy it with little danger. Sailing is actually one of the safer sports around. This chapter will point you in the right direction for developing the necessary awareness so that you can build sensible practice into your sailing.

A very old gentleman, who taught me a great deal about sailing, was fond of saying: 'Always sail with Prudence, my boy. Sail with Prudence!' For a long time I waited for him to introduce me to her. He was still sailing when he was eighty. I never saw him hurry and I never saw him flap. Whatever happened, he always seemed to be in just the right place, ready to deal with the situation. In him, anticipation was an art. This is what safety is about.

I like to separate safety on boats into two aspects: the safety of the boat and the safety of the individual. You could say that individual safety depends on the boat. That is only partially true. Whereas, if the boat falls apart, you will not be particularly safe, the careless sailor can fall out of his boat and the boat can sail on quite unharmed.

Safety of the Boat

If you intend never to sail except as crew, you may think this is not your responsibility. You should have an interest though! You are all in it together.

Contrary to popular belief, being wrecked on the shore is not the greatest danger that can befall a vessel. Fire comes top of the list and hitting, or being hit, by something that floats comes next. These things *can* happen through bad luck. Hitting the shore *only* happens through bad judgement and is far less common.

Fire

If fire occurs ashore you can usually get away from it. Not so at sea. There you normally have to stay and deal with it. Prevention is thus much better than cure. Gas, electricity and fuel, in that order, are the main causes of fires on boats. Care with these three will reduce the risks tremendously.

Gas

Liquefied propane or butane gases which are used for cooking and heating on many boats, are heavier than air. If these gases escape even in small quantities they will fall into the bilges and stay there. They cannot, after all, leak out of the bottom! If nothing is done, subsequent escapes will continue to build up a concentration until enough is present for a spark or flame to explode it. I have seen this happen.

Reduce the risks of gas escape. Turn off at the bottle when it is not in use, and turn off the cooker *only after burning off what is in the pipework.* The gas bottles, including spares, should be stored in a gas-tight locker which drains overboard, not below decks and not in the engine compartment. It is a good idea to assume that leaks *are* taking place and pump out the bilges regularly. A bilge pump will remove gas as well as water. Also, have a proper gas drill and make sure everyone understands and uses it.

Other fuels

All fuels, particularly petrol, are potentially dangerous. Store spare fuel in metal containers, well ventilated and away from both engine and batteries. Personally I prefer not to carry petrol below decks at all.

Diesel engines are so much safer than petrol, and so much more reliable, that I prefer not to have inboard petrol engines. Many boats still do, however, and they do need more safety thinking on the part of their skippers.

Extinguishers

You cannot call the fire brigade at sea! You must therefore make sure you have the right equipment to deal with any fire. As a minimum, you need two fire extinguishers on all but the smallest boats. One, which should be of the compressed gas type for inboard engine fires, and another for fuel, electrical or other fires. For this I prefer the dry powder type. Foam is not the best thing, even on low voltage electrical fires. A fire blanket is best for galley fires and for small fuel fires. Do not forget you have plenty of water available – not for liquid fires though.

The extinguishers should be fitted in positions that can be reached from on deck. Almost all boat fires start below decks. It is essential to get into the open fast if a fire starts, because you have a very limited amount of oxygen in a small cabin. Get outside, then you can fight the fire. Many of the fire extinguishers are potentially poisonous in confined spaces. This will not matter if you are in the open.

Collision

If your boat hits something substantial at sea (and it does not have to be a super tanker) it may get a hole in it. Recently, several cases have been reported of yachts hitting partly submerged containers lost from deck cargoes. I have been very close to this myself and had no advance warning at all. They tend to float at, or just under the surface. Thinking about being holed before it happens and planning what you would do is not morbid or cowardly. It is sensible, seamanlike practice. Planning saves panic and can save lives.

What you will do exactly, depends on where you are hit and how big the hole. Some general ideas can be stated though. First you must stop the water from coming in faster than you can remove it. If you cannot do that, you will need to abandon your vessel and take to the liferaft.

A change to the opposite tack may lift the hole above the water line. Slowing down or stopping will reduce the water pressure if the hole is at or near the bow. Anything which will reduce the intake of water will help. Bedding, bunk cushions or clothing can be stuffed in and are readily available. Jammed in place with bunkboards or anything else hard and handy, this will do the trick for a while.

In modern boats the problem is often getting to the hole. You need to face up to the fact that smashing the cocktail cabinet is better than sinking. Your insurance company will prefer it too! Quite hefty force may be needed, so carry a small axe with you. Once you have controlled the flow you are going to need to make a more effective repair. For this, a saw, a drill with bits, and some self-tapping screws will make life easier.

A further cause of embarrassment can be the loss of a sea cock. If you carry some softwood bungs of the right size to bang into the hole, it is a lot more comfortable than sitting like Hans with your thumb in it. These bungs can also be used to block punctures caused by striking a sharp object. An old bolt or spike in a quay wall for example.

At a course I attended some years ago on damage control, the instructor was discussing the frequency with which old bolts are found sticking out of pilings and posts. 'What would you do', he posed, 'if you were just coming alongside the harbour wall and one of those bolts went right through the side of your boat?'

One wag instantly replied. 'Slap a washer and a nut on it. Then you would be moored *and* secured!' Not quite the answer expected but certainly an example of quick thinking.

Bilge pumps

Bilge pumps are part of your safety equipment, not just for getting rid of rain water that runs off your oilskins and finds its way below decks. If you get holed you will need the pumps. An electric pump can shift more water than a man, and it does not get tired. If the boat gets a bad leak though, the batteries could be under water and the pump may stop.

It is best to have two or more pumps, at least one of which is manual. It is often said that a frightened man with a bucket makes the most efficient pump! Generally a mechanical pump is more effective and less tiring. The main thing is to get the water out, and the more ways you have, the better. Buckets need to have lanyards attached to strong handles so that they do not get lost over the side.

Breakage of gear

Most breakages can be avoided by preventative maintenance. Check things frequently, and repair or replace them if in doubt. This is easier if you have no budget problems. If the choice is between a new spinnaker and replacing a dodgy forestay, the forestay must win. Don't skimp on safety aspects. As crew you cannot do much about this except not to sail in a badly maintained boat. Your life is at stake after all.

Ideally, after any breakage, the boat must be able to stay afloat, move under its own power and go where you want it to. Keeping this in mind you can apply the 'what if' approach. What if a halliard breaks? What if the tiller breaks, the mast falls down . . . and so on. Don't become obsessive about it. The idea is to plan possible solutions. If you can carry spares for the more easily replaced items it does help a lot.

For some of the questions there will be no realistic solution, but you can still plan a course of action. If you decide you will have to cut the mast away, have you got the tools to do that? Do you know how to send a 'Mayday' call? What will you take with you if you have to use the liferaft?

Safety Equipment

The problem with safety equipment is that you hope and expect it will never be used. This means that, once installed, it is often neglected. You need to go for what is necessary, make sure it is looked after and that everybody on board knows how to use it. Once an item is on board, it is easy to forget. Having the right item is no good if no one knows where it is, or what to do with it. Figure 4.1 lists the safety equipment I would want to find on a cruising yacht.

You may argue that some things should not be on the list; that some things are not safety equipment at all. I believe that being able to change your clothes if you get wet, being able to get warm when you

---

Fire Fighting
2 fire extinguishers
1 fire blanket
2 buckets with lanyards

Man-overboard
2 lifebelts with strobe lights
1 Dan buoy (flag marker)
1 boarding ladder
1 light line with quoit

Damage Control
set of softwood bungs (to fit seacock
   holes)
assorted loose ply for patches
assorted self tapping screws
   (bronze nails if wooden boat)

Spares
assorted shackles
assorted clevis pins
light bulbs
fuses
cordage (several sizes)
insulated wire
batteries (to suit torches and
   instruments)
siezing wire
engine spares (maker's pack if possible)

Personal
   (for each member of crew)
1 lifejacket
1 safety harness
1 set of oilskins
1 set of spare clothing
1 sleeping bag

Flares in water tight packs (minimum)
3 hand-held red
3 red parachute rockets
2 orange smoke
3 white hand-held

Tools
1 pair bolt croppers (for cutting rigging)
1 all purpose saw
1 hammer
1 small axe
1 drill (hand or low voltage)
1 set drill bits
1 set spanners to suit engine
1 soft mallet
3 sizes of screwdriver (both cross-head
   and star)
1 hand vice or clamp
1 pair combination pliers
1 pair grip pliers
1 marlin spike with shackle key

Liferaft (size to suit number on board)

Emergency Pack (sometimes called
   a panic bag) comprising:
   fresh water in cans
   emergency rations
   sponge
   first aid kit

Food & Cooking
sufficient food for the expected passage
   time plus 24 hours
spare fuel for cooker
'easy-eat' food e.g. chocolate, nuts,
   biscuits, fruit

First Aid Kit

Fig. 4.1   Safety equipment for a cruising yacht

are cold, and being able to eat when you are hungry, are all part of safety. If you read the report of the enquiry into the Fastnet Race of 1979, you will find that the crews that could not do these things suffered far more problems than those that could.

The idea of my list is to make *you* think by giving you an idea of how *I* think. I may have left off things you would want to include. If you take too much, though, you may need to tow a second boat to carry it all!

Liferaft

If you ever sail out of sight of land you should have a liferaft. Even unsinkable boats can catch fire and burn. An inflated, or part-inflated, dinghy is a poor substitute for a liferaft in bad weather. The liferaft should be large enough to carry the maximum crew but no larger. Rafts are less stable when only partly full. It must be located where it can be launched quickly and where no member of the crew needs to go below decks to get at it.

A liferaft is launched by first attaching the raft's line to a strong point on the boat, then throwing the raft overboard and pulling in the line until the raft inflates. Once inflated it is difficult to recover and costly to repack, so you cannot really practice. Clubs and schools do demonstrations, however, and it is a good idea to get to one if you can.

Liferafts must be serviced every year. They do not last forever. It is expensive to replace them but this must not be neglected.

Flares

Three kinds of pyrotechnics, generally called flares, are used on boats. They are those that warn of your presence, and those that call for assistance, by day and by night. They all have limited life and the expiry date will be marked on them. Peace of mind comes with regular replacement, but keep the ones that are just out of date, because they will probably still work. Much older ones should be properly disposed of, not fired off. I always give my old flares to the Coastguard who will use them for practice.

The *here-I-am* flares give a white light and should be of the hand-held variety. They are for use at night in situations when you need to attract attention to yourself, for example if you think you are about to be run down.

Distress flares for night use are red. They can also be used by day but are not so easily seen. They must only be used in an actual distress situation. Most are the kind that send a parachute rocket up into the sky so that they can be seen from a long distance away. Hand-held red flares are only useful when in sight of a would-be rescuer.

Orange smoke flares are used by day as distress flares because they can be seen more easily. They are either hand-held or of the floating variety intended to be thrown into the sea. Because of this, the vessel in distress must again be in sight of the would-be rescuer. They are particularly useful in helicopter rescues.

Discharging flares

Almost all modern flares are self-igniting but not all are started in the same way. Find out how yours work before you need to use them. They should all be used down wind to avoid setting fire to the boat. Parachute flares are designed to be launched down wind and will climb into the wind to reach their maximum height.

One important rule is NEVER DISCHARGE A DISTRESS FLARE EXCEPT IN A DISTRESS SITUATION, unless the discharge is at a demonstration authorised by HM Coastguard. The emergency services will *always* respond to distress flares and lives can be lost in false alarms.

VHF in emergency

I make no apology for including VHF radio under emergency equipment. With the rapidly reducing visual coastguard service, radio has become an essential on every cruising boat. If you have it you should be capable of using it, at least in an emergency. The Mayday call is the internationally recognised method of broadcasting a distress message. The word comes from the French 'M'aidez!' It should only be used when *the vessel is in grave and imminent danger*. Note these words carefully. It says the vessel, not an individual. It also says imminent. Other classifications of message exist for less serious situations.

The form of the Mayday call should be known by everyone aboard any boat having a two-way radio, and it should be displayed on or near the set. You will find the actual wording in Appendix C. It is important to use the correct words in the correct order since the person receiving your call may not be fluent in English.

Personal Safety

Whilst the ultimate responsibility for the safety of those on board depends on the skipper, common sense dictates that each member of the crew looks after him or herself. You do have a vested interest in staying alive and unhurt.

Lifejackets

On a cruising boat a lifejacket should be available for each person aboard. A buoyancy aid is not a lifejacket because it will not keep an unconscious person afloat unaided, with the face above water. In safety planning, always look to the worst case. Remember that, even when never used, lifejackets have a limited life and need to be tested regularly.

When should they be worn? It is difficult to make hard and fast rules about this. Clearly if you are sitting in the cockpit on a clear calm day, wearing your lifejacket might be considered pessimistic. In fog, at night, when on the foredeck in a gale, you would be a fool to be without it! It is the in-between situations that are difficult.

As a general rule, lifejackets should be worn in any of the following situations: at night, in heavy weather, in a dinghy, by non-swimmers on deck, in fog, when the skipper says so, or if you feel the need for one.

The last two are important. The good skipper should be aware of potential dangers and of the ability of his crew. He must be able to insist on any aspects of safety for the good of all. If you, as a crew member, are nervous without a lifejacket it is sensible to wear one. You know your own limitations better than anyone. The cautious are more likely to survive.

Safety harness

On the principle that it is better to stay with the boat than to be rescued from the sea, I feel that a good safety harness is more important than a lifejacket. It must be a full chest harness and it must fit you. If you borrow one, adjust it to fit as soon as you get it.

One end of the safety line is attached to you, the other to the boat. Both ends are equally important. If you wear the harness and do not attach it, you would be better off without it. A properly equipped boat will have special strong points for harness attachment. It may also have steel wires (jack stays) running the length of the boat so that you can clip on before leaving the cockpit. Use the correct points, not the guard rails which would come away if you fell overboard.

A harness should be worn far more often than it is. It can be restricting and a nuisance but wear it: at night, in heavy weather, in the cockpit when sailing alone, when reefing and when working on the foredeck in stress conditions. Lives of even very experienced sailors have been lost through failure to wear a harness in situations when it should have been worn.

Man overboard!

This is the cry we all hope never to hear in earnest. Equipment must be ready for immediate use all the time in case it does happen. It must be close at hand, near the helm position is best. Anyone who falls overboard will pass behind the boat, the helm will always be manned and the person on the helm is most likely to notice anyone go over.

A lifebelt, with an automatic light for night time, and a flag marker are the first and most urgent items needed. They need to be got over the side immediately so that, together with the shout, everyone will know what has happened and where it has occurred. A head is surprisingly difficult to see at quite short distances, even in near calm water. Give the victim buoyancy, mark his or her position and have crew ready with a line to throw or wrap round the person when you get back; do this and the crisis can be overcome quickly and calmly.

On a practical course you will be taught a method which will show you what to do to get back rapidly to someone in the water. The recovery can be more difficult than getting to the victim, so be sure to learn how it's done. Recovery should also be taught on a practical course. Learn these skills well and practise them often so that you know what to do if you ever need to.

Skippering and Safety

The good skipper is safety conscious but not too obviously so. Most readers of this book will not yet be skippers but it does not hurt to know how to think safety. The skipper must watch for potential hazards and must avoid them. He should make sure that you, as crew, know what to do in any situation. He should keep his crew well fed, warm and rested. He must make sure that all safety equipment is ready for use and in good condition, and that everyone knows how and when to use it. Plan, prepare and practice are the key words in safety.

The skipper needs rest as much as the crew. He cannot be on the go for 24 hours in every day, so he needs the crew to be safety conscious so they can help keep everyone safe. It is up to the skipper to make sure that his crew know how to do this. There is a set of rules which help a great deal. They are discussed in detail in the next chapter.

5

The Rules of the Road

What you will learn

The most important parts of the Collision Avoidance Regulations as they relate to small vessels.
What these rules are likely to mean in practice and how to apply them.
Where to find the complete rules.

By the time you have completed the chapter you will know

Sufficient to understand the Collision Avoidance Regulations so as to be able to apply them sensibly.
How their implications apply to you in relation to other vessels you meet.
You should be aware of the need to be familiar with all these rules.

What you will need

In order to get the most out of this chapter you should have a copy of the Collision Avoidance Regulations available for study. Make sure that the copy you have is up to date. A last year's copy of a Nautical Almanac will contain the regulations.

The system for regulating the behaviour of vessels on the water is like the system used for vehicles on the roads. Indeed, the needs of vessels are somewhat similar to those of road vehicles. They still have to meet, overtake and pass with safety. When meeting or overtaking, the driver of each, be they cars, yachts or whatever, needs to know what the other is going to do. Just as the rules for motor vehicles are based on logic, so are those for vessels.

There are some important differences however. Vehicles on land travel within well defined and clearly visible boundaries; when roads intersect, there are visible signs to indicate which vehicle has priority. And generally vehicles stick to the roads, so when a car or lorry comes to a national boundary a new set of rules may apply but the boundary will remain visibly defined. None of these things is true at sea.

At sea the International Regulations for the Preventing of Collisions at Sea come into operation. These rules have been laid down by the Inter-Governmental Maritime Organization. It has to be an international code because vessels at sea, even yachts, are not always in the territory of one country. Some sea territory belongs to no one country. Vessels are continually changing from the territorial waters of one nation to those of another. If each nation had its own set of rules, chaos would ensue.

In the event of an accident or incident which is the subject of an investigation, any enquiry will take into account whether the vessels involved were obeying the regulations. If either or both of them was not, this would be grounds to be considered in apportioning blame. To sailors this means follow the regulations, or you may be blamed for not doing so. It makes sense, therefore, to learn the 'Collision Regs', as they are often called. I personally dislike this name because they are not regulations *'for'* collisions, they are regulations for *'preventing'* collisions, which is a very different thing.

You can buy the original form if you wish. You will also find them reprinted in most almanacs, but the majority of small-boat sailors use the version published by the RYA which has useful notes on each rule. The current edition is Pamphlet G2/83. I believe that everyone who may be in control of a vessel at sea should have a copy. Have you got one?

From here on I shall call them 'The Rules', because this is the way I want you to regard them. I intend to cover only the areas that are extra important when you start sailing. The rest is up to you. I shall quote rule numbers, not because I want you to learn them parrot fashion, but because I want you to be able to refer quickly to the right place in your copy.

Steering and Sailing Rules (Part B)

Look-outs

The first few rules are concerned with whom they apply to, and are basically definitions. The first rule in Part B is Rule 5 relating to *look-outs*. I think it worth stating in full here:

> Every vessel shall at all times maintain a proper look-out by all available means appropriate in the prevailing circumstances and conditions so as to make a full appraisal of the situation and of the risk of collision.

The RYA booklet says: 'This is a most important rule. If it is not observed, the rest of the rules might as well not exist.' I make no apology for quoting the rule or the comment; I fully agree with both. A skipper should have this rule engraved on his heart!

A good look-out does mean in *all* directions. It is very easy in a boat to look round in the general direction that you are heading and fail *even to notice* a vessel coming up on you from anywhere abaft the beam. Also, in a sailing boat, the arc of view on the lee side, forward of the mast, will often be obscured by the foresail, particularly if it is a low cut one. If this happens, someone must be positioned so that he can cover this blind area and give adequate warning.

There are two particular situations when people often fail to keep good look-outs. The first is when sailing into the wind in cold, wet or very windy conditions. In such conditions, the physical discomfort produced by looking into the wind may discourage anyone from actually doing so.

The other is at night. Night vision is acquired over time. It is the ability to see objects when ambient light levels are low. A single flash of a torch into the face of a look-out, can, and will, reduce his acquired night vision to zero for a period of anything up to ten minutes. Ample time to hit a ship on a closing course!

Look and Listen, particularly in poor visibility. Notice that the rule says 'all available means'. This means radar too, if you have it. It also means that you should make sure that *you* can be seen and heard. Lights, radar reflector, sound signals; these are all in the rules.

Most of these things, if not all, will be mentioned on any practical course, but it does no harm to think of them now. Before we leave look-outs, I would suggest you consider one more thing. There is a difference between *seeing* something and *reacting* to it. This is particularly so when one is tired. The best look-out is one who keeps a frequent, but not continuous watch, and reacts quickly when something comes into view. I would rather have people point out things I have seen, than fail to point out the one which I have not!

Risk of collision

Rule 5, described above, says we are required to assess the risk of collision. Rule 7 makes the point again. It is a reminder and an expansion of the point. In particular, it mentions radar and says that if you have it you *must use it properly*. Many considerations are involved in deciding if a collision is possible, but this rule mentions two in particular. If the relative bearing between your vessel and the suspect, approaching vessel does not change with time, a collision will occur. That is, of course, if neither vessel takes any action. This is vitally important but is not always clear. Figure 5.1 shows why it will happen.

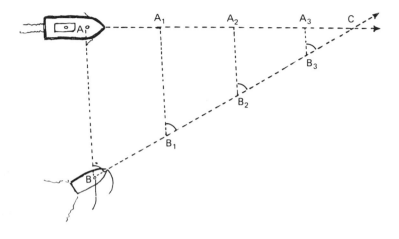

Fig. 5.1   A collision course situation

You are sitting on your boat 'B' and you see boat 'A' getting nearer, so you take a bearing on it with your hand-bearing compass. Since you are getting closer to the other boat, your two courses must cross at some time. The trick is to find out if you will both reach the point where they cross at different times or at the same time. Five minutes later you take a second bearing and it is the same. You check again after another five minutes and still get the same bearing.

At the moment you took the first bearing you were steering your particular course. Vessel 'A' was steering his. During the first five minutes you have moved from B to B1, in the second five from B1 to B2, in the third from B2 to B3 and so on. Meanwhile vessel 'A' has moved from A to A1, to A2 to A3. Since all the bearings you measured are the same, lines AB, A1B1, A2B2 and A3B3, are all parallel. By geometry, one can prove that triangles ABC, A1B1C and so on, are all similar triangles. This means that both vessels are covering their respective tracks to point C in exact proportion and will thus arrive there at the same time. C for collision!

The second point the rule makes is that if the approaching vessel is very large, a super tanker or a tow perhaps, or if you are fairly close already, the bearing may change quite a lot and a risk still exist. The message is, use the compass but be cautious.

'Give way' and 'stand on'

In any meeting situation where a risk of collision exists, one vessel is designated the GIVE WAY vessel and the other is the STAND ON vessel. These terms are quite precise. The give way vessel is the one that is *required by the rules* to take action to avoid the possible collision. The stand on vessel is *required to maintain both course and speed*, i.e. to take no action unless it becomes clear that only an action by the stand on vessel will avoid a collision. This means that there is no such thing as a 'right of way'. Every vessel is required to avoid collisions.

Avoiding collisions

Once we have decided a collision is likely, what do we do to avoid it? Rule 8 makes some suggestions. In simple terms it tells us to:

1 Take any action early and make it sensible action in accordance with the other rules.
2 Make any change of course big enough to be seen.
3 Make sure that any course change made does not introduce another problem.
4 Do not just change, but make sure that you will actually clear, and keep checking until the risk is over.
5 Do remember that you can slow down or stop, as well as change course.

Look at the actual wording of the rule. All these suggestions are sensible, even obvious. But collisions still occur.

To put the rule even more briefly. Keep checking, keep out of the way and make sure the other vessel can see that you are doing so.

The worst thing you can do is to keep making tiny changes in your movements. If you do, the other vessel will find it very hard to know what you are doing and you may actually *cause* a collision.

Who does what

Rule 8 makes it clear, in general, how to avoid collisions. The next few rules, right up to the end of the particular section, lay down, in broad terms, who does what in particular situations. It is for you to learn these rules and I shall not repeat them here. What I will do is to try to make it easier for you to understand the logic behind them. This makes it easier to learn.

The logic

All the rules in this section are based on the idea that it makes sense if the vessel least able to manoeuvre in any situation gives way. Rule 18 lays down a likely sequence which applies in the open sea. The earlier rules apply to specific problems. Rule 19 tells you what to do when you cannot see. The sequence of Rule 18 should be learned. In the following list, each class of vessel gives way to every vessel *lower* in the list:

Power
Sailing
Fishing
Not under command
Restricted in ability to manoeuvre
Constrained by draught

For those who like mnemonics to help them, I suggest: **P**ut **S**afety **F**irst **N**ever **R**isk **C**ollision.

It has the added advantage that, even if you can't remember what the initials stand for it is still a message worth remembering!

The meanings of all the terms used in the list are clearly defined in the rules. For example you, on your yacht, are 'a power driven vessel' if your engine is on and in gear, *even* if you have all your sails full and drawing. Equally, the person who hires a little boat for the day and hangs a mackerel line over the back is not 'a vessel engaged in fishing', nor incidentally, is a true fishing boat when dashing back to port laden after a good day, even though his fishing signal may be welded to the forestay!

Sailing vessels

Rule 12 concerns the conduct of sailing vessels directly. Even on the local boating pond you need to know this rule! Figures 5.2 to 5.6 give examples of the application of the rules relating to sailing vessels. In each of the diagrams, vessel A is the give way vessel and vessel B is the stand on vessel. Again, it is possible to simplify Rule 12 a bit. If you assume that as a helmsperson you will sit on the windward side of the boat, you can say: 'If I am on the right, I am in the right!'

Try it with each situation and you will find it works. Remember though, this really is a gross simplification. There is no substitute for learning the actual rule. The situations are:

    1   For two vessels meeting on opposite tacks, the vessel on port tack gives way. Logic: he can turn to starboard simply by easing sheets. The boat on starboard tack would have to go about.

2   For sailing vessels on the same tack, the windward boat keeps clear. Logic: if they are closing, the windward boat will be sailing with its sails more free. It can harden up or bear away. The other, close on the wind, can only bear away or must go about.

3   If you can't tell which tack the other boat is on and you are on port tack, assume it is on starboard and give way. Logic: he *knows* which tack he is on.

If you remember that, in general, *the correct manoeuvre to avoid a collision is a turn to starboard*, you should be able to see that the rules are so designed as to avoid having to tack. This, of course, is the most difficult manoeuvre for a sailing boat.

Narrow channels and separation schemes

Rules 9 and 10 are concerned with waters where the direction of travel and position when travelling are controlled. In the former case, it is by visible marking and in the latter, by charted boundaries. In general the best advice is to avoid both narrow channels and traffic separation schemes. If you cannot, then keep out of the way.

Think of your small boat as akin to a bicycle on a trunk road. You are very vulnerable and the big stuff can't do much to avoid you. Remember neither you nor the ship bearing down on you has any

Fig. 5.2   Rule 18: 'Power gives way to sail'

Fig. 5.3   Rule 18: 'Power gives way to sail'

Fig. 5.4   Rule 12: 'Windward boat keeps clear'
         Both boats on the same tack

Fig. 5.5   Rule 12: 'Port gives way to Starboard'
Port tack meets starboard tack

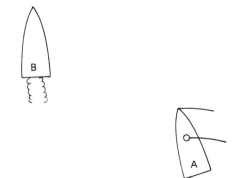

Fig. 5.6   Rule 13: 'Overtaking boat keeps clear'
Even if under sail!

brakes! Traffic separation schemes are more like motorways; you and your bike shouldn't be there, so cross straight and don't get in anybody's way.

Closing situations

Rules 13, 14 and 15 are concerned with the three possible ways that vessels may get closer together, namely, overtaking, meeting head-on and crossing situations.

Overtaking

Overtaking is actually defined as approaching a vessel from a direction more than 22.5 degrees abaft the beam on either side. This is easier to understand in a diagram as shown in Figure 5.6. If you are overtaking, no matter what kind of vessel you are, you must not get in the way of the vessel you are overtaking. Having started to overtake, you remain the overtaking vessel until you are past and clear. You must not cause the overtaken vessel to change course. At the same time, if you are being overtaken, you do not have the right to get in the way of the overtaking vessel by changing course. Be sensible and considerate.

Head-on

Meeting head-on can be unnerving. Broadly the rule says, if you think you may collide head-on, get out of the way by making a turn to starboard (Figure 5.7). It relates, however, to power driven vessels, so if either or both of you are sailing, Rule 12 applies. Remember, two vessels meeting head-on are closing at a rate equal to their combined speeds so action early, rather than late, is called for. The action must be substantial since it must be obvious to the other vessel.

Crossing

If both vessels are under power, the vessel having the other on its starboard side is the give way vessel. This is because a turn to starboard, which is the correct give way action, will mean that the give way vessel passes *behind* the stand on vessel. Figure 5.8 should make this clear. The dotted lines show the progress of each vessel.

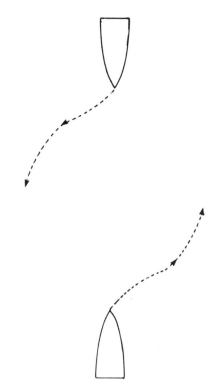

Fig. 5.7 Rule 14: Head-on situation
Both vessels turn to starboard before resuming original course

Remember the basics

It is very important that the two terms, give way and stand on, are understood. The term 'right-of-way' is not used in the rules. You either *give way*, which means change course, slow down or stop, or you *stand on*, which means you make no alteration to course or speed. A little thought should convince you that this makes sense. No one has the right to blast on regardless. Everyone has a duty to avoid collisions. Part B of the rules tells you which action to take in any situation.

Lights and Shapes (Parts C and D)

Parts C and D of the rules are concerned with the lights, shapes and sounds used on, and by, vessels to indicate both what they are, in relation to Rule 18, and also what they are doing. Without these identification marks, it is often surprisingly difficult to decide what a particular vessel is doing.

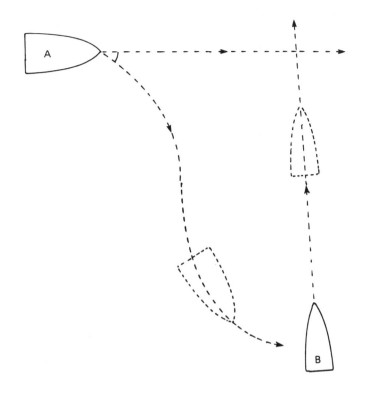

Fig. 5.8 Rule 15: Crossing

Directional lights

The primary set of lights in a vessel are those which tell an observer if it is moving, and in what direction. These are the NAVIGATION LIGHTS. The other lights are always additions to this basic set. Figure 5.9 shows the lights required on a yacht which is capable of motoring. These are the minimum lights needed by a power driven vessel over seven metres long. Rule 21 defines these lights and gives their ARCS OF VISIBILITY. If you relate these arcs to the overtaking rule, you will grasp the logic of them.

The actual positions and numbers of lights are determined, quite reasonably, by the size of vessel. A big vessel will not only have more power available for its lights, it will also need to be identified earlier and more precisely!

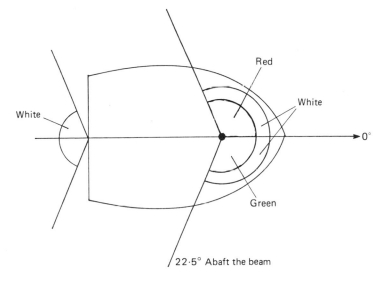

Fig. 5.9   Navigation light sectors

Combined lights

A vessel under 20 metres long can have the red and green sidelights combined in one lantern. A vessel under 12 metres in length, including a sailing vessel, can have these and the stern light combined in one lantern. This represents a considerable saving of precious battery power. The so-called 'steaming light' must always be a separate lantern because it must be vertically separated from the navigation lights. This will not matter so much because if you are motoring (steaming), the engine will be running to charge the batteries.

Sailing lights and shape

A sailing vessel, when sailing, only shows sidelights and stern light. By day, a vessel using sails *and* engine must display a cone shape point down in the fore part of the boat.

Extra lights

The first 'extra' light is the second masthead light which is a requirement only on vessels of over 50 metres. It is quite useful, when confronted by a vessel that size, to be able to say, 'it is pointing at me if the masthead lights are seen above each other'. The red and green sidelights, which should both be visible in this situation, are not always easy to see in amongst the ship's other lights.

Rules 23 to 29 tell you about the extra lights and shapes to be carried by vessels that are restricted in their movements in some way. It is up to you to learn these in time. If, when you start night sailing, you regard anything with lights, other than navigation lights, as something to be given way to, you will not go far wrong. You may spend a lot of time getting out of the way but it is better than being run down!

Fishing vessels represent a particular hazard for several reasons. Often they do not have the expected lights or shapes. Sometimes, when gear is out, they have very limited ability to manoeuvre and also very erratic movement. Also, their gear can extend some considerable distance from the sides of, as well as behind, the boat. Add to this the fact that often, when the whole crew is engaged in hauling in the nets, an inadequate watch is kept; it is as well to give them a wide berth and to continue to watch them until well past.

Once in the North Sea I slowed down to let a trawler on port cross my bows, only to have him make a sharp turn to starboard just after doing so, thus putting me between him and his trawl!

Anchored vessels

The lights to be displayed when at anchor are given in Rule 30. By day, any vessel at anchor must show a ball shape 'where it can best be seen'. This is just as important for a yacht as for a large vessel. It is often difficult for someone on the bridge of a large, fast moving vessel to tell if a small yacht is actually moving or not.

Sound Signals

Manoeuvres

The manoeuvre and warning signals are in Rule 34. Those for restricted visibility are in Rule 35. The most important are given here. They all consist of long blasts, short blasts or a mixture. A short blast is actually a blast of up to one second, so can seem long. A long blast must actually sound for between four and six seconds.

The meanings of the short blast signals are as follows:

Number of blasts	Meaning
1	I intend to turn to starboard
2	I intend to turn to port
3	My engines are going astern
	Note: He may just be slowing down, not necessarily going backwards.
4	I am a pilot
5	I do not understand your intentions
	Notes: this signal is often used for 'Get out of my way!'

Warnings

One prolonged blast means 'I am here'. It is used by power driven vessels in bad visibility, or when rounding an obstruction and wishing to make one's presence known.

Two prolonged blasts together in bad visibility mean 'I am here and not moving'. One prolonged blast, followed by two short blasts, is actually the Morse letter 'D'. It means, 'I am manoeuvring with difficulty', and may be used in bad visibility by anything other than an unrestricted power driven vessel. It is the signal you would use if sailing in fog.

Distress

In addition to the rules for operation of vessels, Annexe IV to the rules lists a number of signals which are recognised as distress signals. Any of these may be used to attract attention in a genuine distress situation as described in Chapter 3. Figure 5.10 gives the signals on this list that could be used by a yacht.

(a)   A gun or similar signal at intervals of about 1 minute
(b)   Continuous sounding of a fog signal
(c)   The firing of red rocket flares
(d)   The sending of SOS . . . — — — . . . in light by Morse Code
(e)   The 'Mayday' signal by radio
(f)   The letters NC by flag
(g)   The flying of a square flag under or over a ball shape
(h)   An orange smoke signal
(i)   The repeated raising and lowering of outstretched arms
(j)   The use of an Emergency Position Indicating Radio Beacon (EPIRB)

Fig. 5.10   Distress signals

Reflections

I have covered the more important points from the rules in this chapter. You will need to learn them all in time. If you can remember the main ideas, you can fill in the details later. For your own safety, and the safety of others, you should make these rules a priority in your study before going to sea.

6

Starting to Navigate

What you will learn

How to understand the information given in charts.
   What instruments you will need in order to be able to record your progress.
   The basis equipment necessary to measure your progress, in particular the compass and the log.
   The limitations of these instruments.
   Which publications are needed to make navigation possible.

By the time you have completed the chapter you will know

How charts and other publications can be used to find your way about.
   The kind of information that can be found from a chart and how to start interpreting the signs.
   You will have to have some knowledge of the instruments used for navigation and how they are used.

What you will need

Before you start:
   Any chart; an old one will do.
   A Nautical Almanac, preferably a current one or that for the previous year. Last year's edition can often be bought very cheaply and will be adequate for study of this chapter. Or borrow one from a friend.
   Later on:
   Admiralty publication 5011 (for chart symbols).
   A pilot book (borrowed from your local library).

It has often been said that navigation is an art not a science. It is an art because far too many things in navigation are unpredictable for it to become a science. It is the art of knowing where you are and how to get to where you want to go.

Some basic essentials are needed even to start to navigate a boat. First, a set of maps (sea maps are called charts) and the means to measure and record on them. Next you need to know how you are moving in relation to the chart. To find out how you are *actually* moving you need a source of information about all the variables that affect a vessel's movement on the sea. Do not forget that the water moves over the sea bed whilst you move on it. For yachting purposes, a nautical almanac will provide all such information in one volume. Direction and distance are the basis of movement measurement and for these you will need a compass and a log.

Charts

Even if you are very familiar with an area you will still need maps.

In the United Kingdom, Admiralty Charts are the water equivalent of Ordnance Survey maps. The authority for the information on all charts of British waters is The Hydrographer to the Navy. He is also the authority for charts of many other areas of the world. Admiralty Charts are used to publish the information the Hydrographic Department collects. Their study can be fascinating as well as informative. Have a look at one carefully when you have plenty of time. See when it was published, where and when the information in it was found. Surveys of some areas are surprisingly old, but are still of value. Many nations have their own charting authorities, and ways of presenting chart information vary from country to country.

Other publishers produce charts more specifically for yachting, but their information still comes from The Hydrographer.

Chart symbols

To understand all the information on an Admiralty Chart you will need the key. That key is the booklet called Chart 5011. It lists all the symbols and terms used on charts including such exotica as coral reefs and palm trees, as well as more immediately useful things like how to find the depth of water and which rocks might be a danger. Figure 6.1 shows just one page from this booklet.

Before you start any serious navigation you should get hold of your own copy of Chart 5011 and start learning the more important symbols. Do not be put off by the large number of them. Start with the dangers, then with the information about depth and bottom, and so

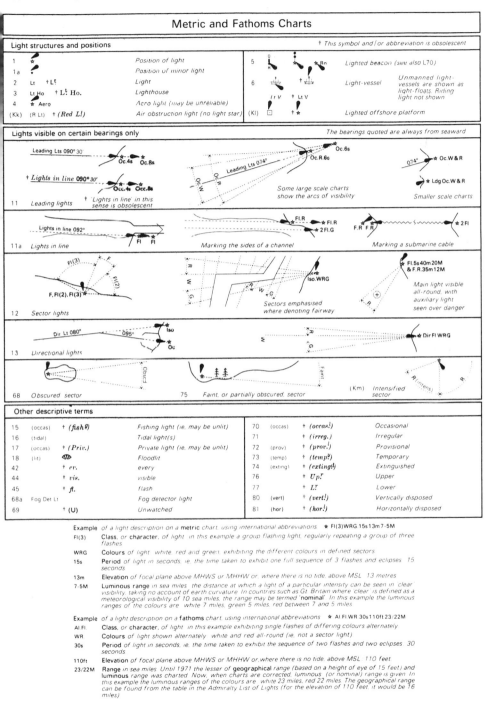

Fig. 6.1 A page from Chart 5011

build up your knowledge. If you practise with an old chart you will soon find that you can recognise all the more common symbols. Many are just abbreviations or little pictures of the real thing.

Information

The kinds of information available from charts fall into distinct categories. In Chart 5011 the categories are given single letter codes for ease of reference. The categories can be grouped into three types. These are: coastal features and other things on land, things that are under the sea, and those which are either floating on it or which come through the surface.

Apart from black and white, only four colours are used on Admiralty Charts. Yellow is used for things always above the surface such as the land, the tops of rocks or islands. Blue is used for land always under the water, and green for land which may or may not be covered, depending on the tide. Magenta is used for such things as boundary lines, notes and to indicate lights.

Blue is used for water only when it is shallow. A big ship will try to keep out of the areas charted in blue, whilst much of your sailing will be done within these areas. The shallower contours are marked with continuous black lines, usually up to about 30 metres. Depths are shown in black, in metres, with a subscript figure representing decimetres against depths below 20 metres.

Chart correcting

One of the great advantages of using Admiralty Charts (or any other national system) is the full correction service that is provided. Each week the Hydrographic Office publishes a list which includes any changes to information on their charts, as well as to their other publications such as *Sailing Directions* and *Lists of Radio Signals*.

These lists, called *Admiralty Notices to Mariners*, are available free from such places as chart agents, Customs Offices etc. Twice annually a *Cumulative List*, and once a year a *Summary Of All Notices In Force*, are published. These publications cover the whole world. More useful to yachtsmen are the quarterly lists, called *Small Craft Editions of Notices to Mariners*, giving only those changes likely to be of interest to small craft users in European waters. These quarterly lists are much quicker to use but must be paid for.

It is important to keep your charts up to date and to check that any chart you are using has been corrected. By custom, all corrections are made in purple ink. Each one is listed in the bottom margin when made. It is thus an easy matter to check that they have been done. Figure 6.2 shows an example of a corrected chart.

Projections

Because the chart represents the curved surface of the world as a flat, two-dimensional surface, the picture you see when you look at a chart is somewhat distorted. Two main methods of projecting the curved surface onto a flat paper are used: Mercator for charts covering large areas and Gnomonic for small areas such as harbours. The techniques are not important but the effects are. Mercator projection means that all lines of latitude and longitude are drawn on the chart straight and at right angles. This makes working on these charts easier, but measuring needs care. This is because the scale in the Mercator system is not linear. It changes slightly as you move up or down the chart. A few simple rules help. These are:

1 Always make measurements on the latitude scale, i.e. using the vertical margins.
2 For accurate measurement, always use the part of the latitude scale that includes the latitude of the point of interest.
3 One minute of one degree of latitude equals one nautical mile.

On Gnomonic charts the lines are not actually straight, but over the small distances involved they can be treated as if they were. Most of your plotting on Gnomonic charts will be in or about harbour areas where you will find it causes no difficulty.

Tools of the Trade

When working on charts it is necessary to make a record of your progress at regular intervals. To do this means drawing on the chart. A soft pencil should always be used. This makes it easier to clean off with the least damage to the surface. The best grade is a 2B which is hard enough to be able to draw fine lines yet soft enough to be able to rub off easily. Pencils must be kept sharp and all lines must be drawn lightly. More is said on this subject in Chapter 9.

Drawing instruments

You will need to be able to measure angles and distances and to move these angles and distances about on the chart. Distances are best

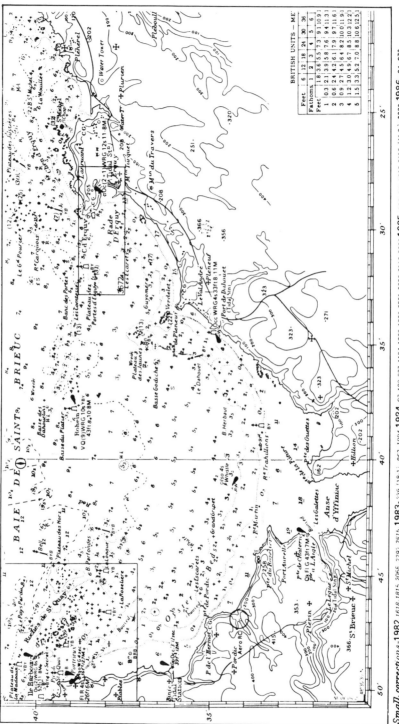

Fig. 6.2 Chart corrections (Chart 2669)

measured and transferred using dividers. The crossover type are easiest since they can be set with one hand only. On a small vessel a pair between six and eight inches (150–200 millimetres) long is best. To measure and mark angles, a special kind of protractor is used against which a line can be drawn at any chosen angle.

The most common are the square Portland or Douglas type, illustrated in Figure 6.3, or one of the patent versions having an extension arm that can be rotated. Most are easy to use once you have studied the directions and practised a little.

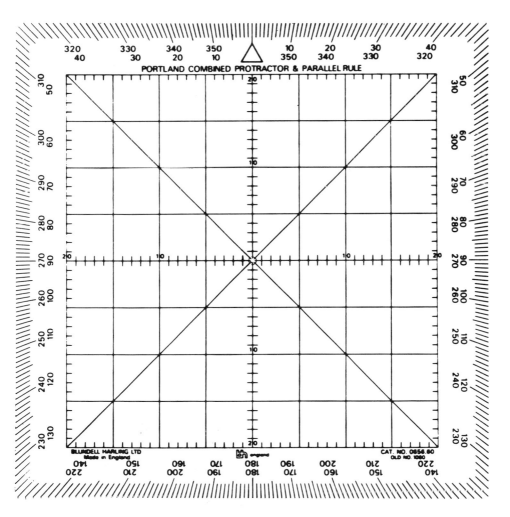

Fig. 6.3 The Portland protractor

Using the Portland protractor

Directions on how to use a square protractor are given on the wallet in which it is sold. When the arrow head is placed so that it points in any particular direction, the sides are parallel to the line of the arrow. When the centre of the protractor is placed on any vertical line on the chart, the angle by which the protractor is rotated away from North can be read from the *inner* scale against that line and a bearing at that angle can be drawn against either side of the protractor.

When using the outer scale, the centre is placed over a point of interest with the protractor aligned with the North/South lines. The direction of any line drawn from the point of interest can then be read on the outer scale. A line can be drawn at any bearing from the point of interest by aligning the protractor North/South and marking the required angle against the outer scale. The line is then drawn joining the point of interest to this mark.

The many patent types that have been devised are too numerous to mention here. These can be examined in any good chandler's but it is best to start with simple instruments. Many of my students have found the Breton Plotter, shown in Figure 6.4, particularly useful. It has the advantage that VARIATION can be set on it by means of a rotating adjustment. Variation is explained later in this chapter.

If you use Admiralty Charts it is possible to work with parallel rules alone to transfer angles, since at least two compass roses are drawn on each chart. This method is not too easy on a lively yacht and needs practice. It is less common now than it used to be, but many sailors still swear by it.

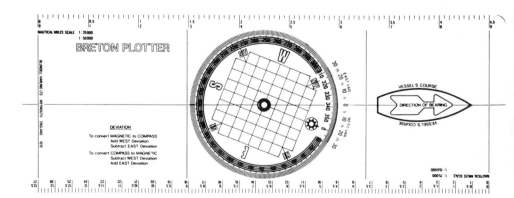

Fig. 6.4 Breton Plotter

Publications

Useful as charts are, they cannot give us all the information that we need or they would become too crowded. As mentioned earlier, the best places for the yachtsman to find extra information are in nautical almanacs and in pilot books or *Admiralty Sailing Directions*.

Nautical almanacs provide all sorts of detailed information on movements of tides, sun rise and set, harbour plans, dangers and marks and a lot more beside. They also give abridged versions of sailing directions, lists of lights and the like. Other useful publications will be mentioned in later chapters.

Almanacs

The most popular almanacs are the *MacMillan and Silk Cut*, and *Reed's*. Both are readily available. For winter practice, you should try to get hold of an old one. The current year's edition can normally be purchased for about a quarter of the published price from about September onwards. You will need a current edition for any real life navigation, but an old one can provide you with a huge fund of information whilst learning.

Pilot books

The almanac has in it much of the information that would otherwise need to be gained from several books. It does not give all you need, though. The original pilot books were private records and used to be jealously guarded volumes, added to and amended by their owners as they gained knowledge of such things as tides, channels, ports and harbours. Nowadays the people who collect such information publish their knowledge and there are few areas for which you can not find a suitable book.

Sailing Directions

Sailing Directions are Hydrographic Office publications and contain a wealth of information. Since they are primarily intended for naval vessels, they sometimes miss out things useful to yachtsmen that pilot books include.

Compasses

To mark your direction of travel on the chart means first knowing what that direction is. The magnetic compass has been used to find directions for many thousands of years. It is still the most important instrument for the small boat sailor. Any well equipped yacht will have at least two. One is used for steering and the other for finding the direction to, or from, the land and sea marks seen as one progresses. On a passage such marks are used to find the boat's position.

Steering compass

The steering compass is fixed to the boat in the force and aft line. Thus, in order to turn this compass, the whole boat must be turned. Since the compass needle always points North/South, the bearing read from the compass is the direction in which the boat is pointing, referred to as the ship's heading. Clearly it is very important that the compass is correctly fixed exactly on the fore and aft line.

Two main types of steering compass are common, 'edge-read' and 'binnacle'. Nowadays the edge-read type is the usual one fitted since many people find it easier to use and, in tiller-steered boats, it is also much easier to position. The edge-read compass is ball shaped and fits into an upright bulkhead. The scale is drawn on a vertical surface so as to be easily read from a sitting position. A built-in light is provided for night use.

The other common type, the binnacle compass, is the traditional compass meant to be read from above. The binnacle is actually the pedestal that houses a cover in which this compass is mounted. It too can be fitted with a light and often has a moveable ring, or bezel, so that a course, once decided upon, can be set by turning the ring.

Hand bearing compass

It is not always convenient to point the boat at every object from which you want a bearing! For taking bearings on things other than straight ahead, a hand-held compass is used. Many designs are found but increasingly people are tending to use the small prismatic type. These, often set in a rubber protective mounting, are light, robust and easy to use. A beta-light is fitted for night use. The prism allows you to use the compass by looking straight along the top at the object. The prism also magnifies the scale. These features all make reading easier.

Damping

DAMPING is an important feature of any compass, but particularly so for a marine hand compass. Damping is the ability of the compass card to come to rest when the compass is moved. A compass with too little damping can be almost impossible to use on all but the calmest sea. One with too much will be slow to react to small changes and can give rise to inaccurate readings.

Variation

Remember a compass needle always lies North/South, whatever direction the compass is turned. Thus, the needle gives an indication of the difference between the direction in which the compass is pointed and the direction of the earth's magnetic poles. This is called a relative bearing. Unfortunately the positions of these poles are not constant. The poles that are used by chart makers are called true poles.

The magnetic poles move fairly slowly about the true poles. Fortunately the movements are fairly predictable and can be calculated in advance. This information is recorded on charts as VARIATION. The actual value at a particular place is shown on each of the compass roses on the chart. The year that the variation was measured is given with an indication of how it is expected to change. Allowance must be made for it when putting bearings taken with the compass onto the chart.

If the variation is in a westerly direction, as it is around the British Isles at the present time, it has the effect of rotating the compass in an anti-clockwise direction. This 'increases' the value of the measured angle so that, to find the true bearing, the variation must be subtracted from the measured value.

I find the mnemonic 'mag to grid get rid', useful. It means to convert from a magnetic bearing to one using the grid lines of the chart, get rid of, or subtract, the variation. This only works when the variation is West, however, so you may be happier with: 'Variation East, compass least, variation West, compass best'. The main thing is to get it correct *every* time.

Deviation

Compasses are subject to a further error which needs to be considered. This is the problem of DEVIATION. Any metal object containing iron or conducting electricity will have a magnetic field associated with it.

Such fields will cause a compass needle to swing away from the earth's field. Most of the time these fields are very small and are often self-cancelling, but on a boat we need to know what effect they are having.

The most common causes of deviation are the engine and the electrical wiring. Some things, such as the loudspeaker of a radio and any instruments which have strong magnets in them, need to be positioned well away from the compass. It is possible to find the deviation on a compass in a particular boat by taking a series of bearings on different headings and comparing them with known bearings from the chart. This is how the deviation card (Figure 6.5) on

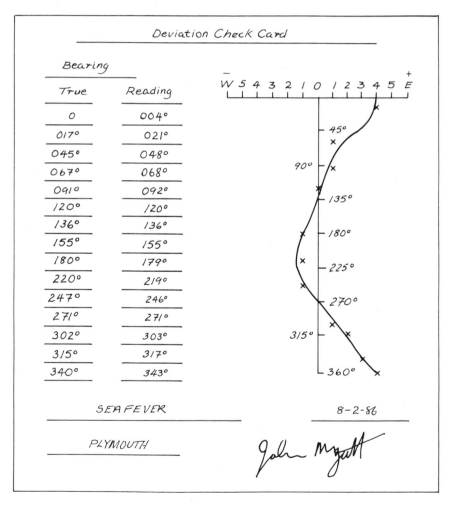

Fig. 6.5   Deviation check card

my boat was produced. Deviation in the steering compass can be reduced, or often eliminated, but the special knowledge of a compass adjuster is needed. How to take deviation into account is discussed in Chapter 9.

All compasses are subject to deviation but, with handbearing compasses unlike steering compasses, deviation will vary randomly since it will depend on where in the boat the compass is used. The best way to reduce this problem is to check against a known bearing with the boat on different headings, then try to find a position in the boat from which you can take bearings at which errors are minimal.

The Log

Early in this chapter I said that the two fundamental things the navigator needs to know are *direction* and *distance*. The compass gives us direction. Distance is measured with a log. Modern log instruments also measure the boat speed, but the most important thing is distance.

In bygone days sailors would measure the speed of the boat by throwing a log of wood over the bow of the boat and finding how long it took to reach the stern. From this they could calculate the distance travelled. Later the log was attached to a piece of string with knots tied at set intervals. This saved logs! It also meant that when the log was thrown over, by counting the number of knots that passed through the hand in a given time, the speed could be calculated more accurately and thence the distance travelled. This is the origin of the terms 'log' and 'knot' we use today.

Log types

The search for accuracy continues. Modern logs use the same basic principle but in a much more sophisticated way. They also measure constantly rather than occasionally, thus giving much more accurate results. Logs are grouped into two types, based on where they sense the movement of the boat through the water. In one system the sensor is fitted so that it pokes through a hole in the bottom of the boat's hull. In the other the sensor is trailed behind the boat and connected by wires or a cord to the reading instrument.

Both systems have their supporters. The 'in-hull' type is easier since it only needs to be switched on, whilst the trailing log must be 'streamed' and taken in again each time. Trailing logs can be cut off by propellers and can snag on the bottom if moving very slowly in shallow water, so they need to be recovered before mooring or manoeuvering in confined spaces! The trailed log, however, is inherently more accurate, and for this reason alone is most popular with long distance sailors.

Relative movement

Whichever kind of log is fitted in your boat it will only measure the distance travelled through the water. The water moves as well as the boat, so to find how the boat has moved in relation to the land, we need to know how the water moves. This is just as true when measuring direction. How we do this is discussed in the next two chapters.

7

Tides: The Ups and Downs

_____ ⚓ _____

What you will learn

What causes the tides and how they affect boat movements.
 The factors that need to be considered in tidal calculations.
 How to predict what will happen.

By the time you have completed the chapter you will know

Why changes in tidal heights occur and how to anticipate them.
 How to calculate the tidal height at a particular place and time.

What you will need before you start

A soft (2B) pencil and a ruler or straight edge.
 Preferably but not essential, the Nautical Almanac you used in Chapter 6.

Shakespeare wrote: 'There is a tide in the affairs of men'. King Canute found that even kings were subject to the rule that 'time and tide wait for no man'. The nature and causes of tides have interested man since he first noticed their existence. For sailors, they are particularly important. Yet, on all the courses I have taught, the problem of tides causes most difficulty to most people. When I talk to other instructors they tell me the same.

Understanding the movements of the sea is crucial to navigation, if not to sailing on it. For this reason I have devoted two whole chapters to the subject in order to unravel the mystery. It's easy when you know how!

What are tides?

Gravity

Everything on earth and in space has, and is subject to, the force of gravity. What gravity *is* does not matter to us but its *effects* are very important. Isaac Newton, who wrote down the rules that govern gravity, made the point that, if a force is applied to anything that is free to move, it will move until the force stops. The huge mass of water that covers our world is, to a very large extent, free to move.

Spring and neap tides

Each heavenly body has its own force of gravity, the moon, the sun and the planets all have their effects. The forces of gravity that are applied to the sea, apart from that of the earth which stops the whole lot from floating off, originate in space. The moon's is the strongest of these forces because it is closest to the earth. The sun is next because of its huge mass. The planets have only a very small effect.

If solar and lunar forces are working together, the combined pull will be strongest and we will get tides with the highest highs and lowest lows. When the major two forces are not working together we get lower high tides and higher low tides. These two conditions are called spring and neap tides respectively. The height difference between a high and a low tide is called the range.

The reason the water moves backwards and forwards is that the earth (and the moon, sun and planets) are all spinning and rotating round each other, so the direction of pull keeps changing. Because we can predict where the sun, moon and planets will be at any particular time, we can also predict the directions and strengths of their respective pulls, and thus what their combined effects will be on the sea.

Local difference

Different parts of the world, even parts quite close together, get different tides. In order to understand this we can use a model.

Suppose you are sitting in your bath half-full of water. You now start to swish your hands (apply a force) backwards and forwards. Very quickly the water starts to move with your hands. If you time your swishes, so that each time the water changes direction you give it even a small push the way it is going, it will soon build up enough height at the ends of the bath to start slopping over.

If your timing gets out of step with the pendulum action of the water, called its natural oscillation, the maximum height will rapidly decrease as the water tries to get into step with your hands. The natural oscillation is a function of the length of the bath. If your bath was longer, the water would take longer to reach the end of the bath and start coming back to you. You would need a different rate of hand movement to keep it going.

Each gravitational pull has a fixed pattern and the size of a particular sea (length of bath) is also fixed. Thus, the gravitational force is unlikely ever to exactly match the size of a sea. In fact it does not quite match in any case, and matches pretty badly in some cases. Hence, where the force is applied at *about* the right time a big range results. When it is way out of time a small range, or even no change, occurs. Incidentally, if the force was applied exactly at the right time on each oscillation, the tide height would continue to get higher and higher, just as in the bath, and eventually the sea would leap right over the shore onto the land!

Range, height and stream

Let us now get back into the bath again. Start swilling the water gently back and forth. What happens to the height at different places in the bath? In the middle where the swishing is taking place, the height hardly changes because the water is free to move. At the ends the height changes are large because the ends of the bath stop the horizontal movement of the water, and it piles up. The movement is then reflected back as the level drops again. We have created a single wave which moves backwards and forwards along the bath.

What about the speed of horizontal movement? At the ends of the bath where the water meets a solid surface, there can be no horizontal movement at all unless it spills right over, only movement up and down. In the middle, where the height change is least, the water must be moving at its fastest horizontally. If we think of each sea as a huge bath it is easy to realise that the same thing will be true. The main differences are: that the sides of the sea are neither smooth nor parallel, the bottom is not level or smooth, the ends are not often totally closed.

When a wave is created in a container partly open at the ends, it will not all be reflected back but will still travel backwards and forwards giving changes in level depending on the direction of the pull. This is really what it is all about. The tide is a big wave which moves backwards and forwards across the sea.

The differences in container shape will not stop the grand design. They will simply cause local effects. You are an island in your bath. What happens to the flow around you? These local effects are very important to sailors. The sea is a very big bath, so that tidal effects are much more pronounced both near the shore and in the narrow sections.

On the basis of what has been said so far it is possible to make some predictions:

1 The speed of flow, called the stream, in relation to height changes will be different depending on how far from the ends we are.
2 The rate of stream will be different in different places. Where the stream gets narrower it will also get faster.
3 The height changes will be greater if the flow reaches a dead-end after moving quickly.
4 When the stream flows round an island it will divide and rejoin.
5 The stream, after rejoining, will be disturbed if the distances travelled by each part are not the same.
6 The water, at or near the solid boundary, will tend to be slowed down and diverted by uneven surfaces.
7 The height changes and stream rates will change as the forces causing them change.

There are two other forces that can affect the pattern. These are largely unpredictable and so can sometimes upset the system. They are:

1 Changes in air flow over the surface which can cause changes in the stream rate and direction, and even the range.
2 Changes in air pressure which can cause quite large changes in the range.

We shall come back to all these ideas again. But now we are ready to get out of the bath for a while.

Some terminology

Much of the information on charts and in pilot books is related to tide heights. Figure 7.1 shows all the relevant terms that are related to tide height. You should notice that the height of things above water is related to the level at mean high water springs whilst those below are related to chart datum which is, to all intents and purposes, the lowest tide you are likely to get.

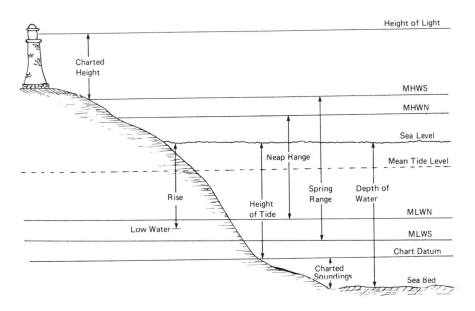

Fig. 7.1 Terms used in tidal data

Using the Predictions

Standard ports

Having established that, although we can make predictions, the height and rate of flow of the tide will be different at different times and places, we now need a system to organise the predictions and where to use them. The system used is to have a series of standard ports for which accurate forecasts are made. These are fairly evenly distributed round the coasts except when a particular area has very unusual tides. In such situations, standard ports may be quite close together. Portsmouth and Southampton are examples; the Isle of Wight causes very abnormal tides.

Secondary ports

It is not sensible or practical to produce predictions for too many standard ports. After all, every prediction has to be recorded and published. First this is done in the Admiralty Tide tables, some parts of which are reproduced in the almanacs. With a very large number of standard ports, these books would become far too big to be useful since not only each place, but each day, is different. In any case, many places close to each other will have almost the same tides. Small places, and places where the information is not very different from a standard port, are therefore treated as secondary ports. The tidal information for these places is recorded in the tables and in the almanacs as a set of differences from the nearest similar standard port. Figure 7.3 shows an example of this.

Using the almanac

To make the last two paragraphs easier to understand, try working through the following:

Extracting the information

Figure 7.2 shows part of the information for the standard port of Dover during 1986. You can see the predicted times of high and low water are given for each tide together with the heights in metres. Before going on, try to decide when in June a spring tide occurred.

The greatest range is found on the 24th when the high water at 12.35 is 6.50 metres, followed by a low water at 20.05 of only 0.80 metres. This is a spring tide. Neap tides are on the 15th and 30th when the range is very small by comparison.

Secondary corrections

Suppose we want to go not to Dover, but to Ramsgate. If you have a copy of *Macmillan and Silk Cut Almanac* look up Ramsgate for yourself. Look at a few other places and notice how the information is presented. If you do not have a copy, the information you will need can be found in Figure 7.3.

Secondary port information

Below the information about charts for the area you will see the sub-heading 'Tides'. The first piece of information gives the difference between the time of high water at the secondary port and at Dover. All tides in the Almanac are related to Dover. The usefulness of this will become more apparent later. The difference in this case is +20 minutes and should be added to the Dover time.

The letters ML stand for mean level. This is the average height the tide reaches above chart datum (see Figure 7.1).

ENGLAND, SOUTH COAST - DOVER

LAT 51°07'N   LONG 1°19'E

TIME ZONE GMT   TIMES AND HEIGHTS OF HIGH AND LOW WATERS   YEAR 1986

MAY

	TIME	M		TIME	M
1 TH	0404 / 1130 / 1633	5.5 / 1.8 / 5.4	**16** F	0258 / 1027 / 1545 / 2259	5.3 / 1.9 / 5.3 / 1.9
2 F	0005 / 0532 / 1250 / 1801	1.7 / 5.2 / 1.9 / 5.2	**17** SA	0419 / 1123 / 1704	5.1 / 2.1 / 5.3
3 SA	0130 / 0716 / 1412 / 1933	1.6 / 5.3 / 1.7 / 5.4	**18** SU	0004 / 0550 / 1236 / 1819	1.9 / 5.1 / 2.1 / 5.4
4 SU	0249 / 0820 / 1521 / 2030	1.4 / 5.6 / 1.4 / 5.7	**19** M	0124 / 0656 / 1355 / 1920	1.7 / 5.4 / 1.9 / 5.7
5 M	0353 / 0907 / 1620 / 2112	1.1 / 5.8 / 1.2 / 6.0	**20** TU	0234 / 0748 / 1500 / 2011	1.4 / 5.7 / 1.6 / 6.1
6 TU	0447 / 0942 / 1708 / 2149	0.9 / 6.0 / 1.1 / 6.2	**21** W	0334 / 0836 / 1556 / 2057	1.1 / 6.1 / 1.3 / 6.4
7 W	0530 / 1014 / 1746 / 2226	0.9 / 6.1 / 1.1 / 6.3	**22** TH	0426 / 0921 / 1647 / 2142	0.9 / 6.3 / 1.1 / 6.6
8 TH	0605 / 1048 / 1812 / 2301	1.0 / 6.2 / 1.1 / 6.4	**23** F	0513 / 1007 / 1734 / 2228	0.8 / 6.5 / 0.9 / 6.7
9 F	0632 / 1125 / 1836 / 2336	1.0 / 6.3 / 1.1 / 6.4	**24** SA	0601 / 1057 / 1822 / 2318	0.7 / 6.6 / 0.9 / 6.7
10 SA	0656 / 1200 / 1904	1.0 / 6.2 / 1.0	**25** SU	0649 / 1149 / 1912	0.7 / 6.6 / 0.8
11 SU	0008 / 0726 / 1231 / 1938	6.3 / 1.0 / 6.2 / 1.1	**26** M	0010 / 0740 / 1242 / 2002	6.6 / 0.7 / 6.5 / 0.8
12 M	0034 / 0758 / 1259 / 2013	6.1 / 1.0 / 6.0 / 1.2	**27** TU	0104 / 0832 / 1333 / 2054	6.4 / 0.9 / 6.3 / 0.9
13 TU	0057 / 0832 / 1326 / 2049	6.0 / 1.2 / 5.9 / 1.4	**28** W	0159 / 0927 / 1420 / 2150	6.2 / 1.1 / 6.1 / 1.1
14 W	0126 / 0905 / 1359 / 2127	5.8 / 1.4 / 5.7 / 1.6	**29** TH	0253 / 1024 / 1512 / 2251	5.9 / 1.4 / 5.9 / 1.3
15 TH	0205 / 0943 / 1444 / 2207	5.5 / 1.7 / 5.5 / 1.8	**30** F	0352 / 1125 / 1610 / 2354	5.6 / 1.6 / 5.7 / 1.5
			31 SA	0502 / 1228 / 1719	5.4 / 1.7 / 5.5

JUNE

	TIME	M		TIME	M
1 SU	0102 / 0625 / 1333 / 1836	1.5 / 5.4 / 1.8 / 5.6	**16** M	0504 / 1150 / 1730	5.4 / 1.9 / 5.7
2 M	0212 / 0730 / 1439 / 1941	1.5 / 5.5 / 1.7 / 5.7	**17** TU	0034 / 0608 / 1259 / 1832	1.6 / 5.5 / 1.9 / 5.8
3 TU	0315 / 0820 / 1536 / 2032	1.4 / 5.6 / 1.6 / 5.9	**18** W	0142 / 0707 / 1409 / 1930	1.5 / 5.7 / 1.7 / 6.0
4 W	0409 / 0905 / 1624 / 2117	1.3 / 5.8 / 1.5 / 6.0	**19** TH	0247 / 0802 / 1514 / 2025	1.4 / 5.9 / 1.6 / 6.2
5 TH	0451 / 0946 / 1701 / 2159	1.3 / 5.9 / 1.5 / 6.1	**20** F	0348 / 0857 / 1614 / 2118	1.2 / 6.1 / 1.4 / 6.3
6 F	0525 / 1026 / 1733 / 2238	1.3 / 6.1 / 1.4 / 6.2	**21** SA	0447 / 0953 / 1715 / 2213	1.1 / 6.3 / 1.2 / 6.4
7 SA	0554 / 1105 / 1805 / 2316	1.2 / 6.2 / 1.3 / 6.2	**22** SU	0546 / 1049 / 1812 / 2309	1.0 / 6.4 / 1.0 / 6.5
8 SU	0627 / 1142 / 1842 / 2350	1.1 / 6.3 / 1.2 / 6.1	**23** M	0645 / 1144 / 1910	0.9 / 6.5 / 0.9
9 M	0703 / 1214 / 1920	1.1 / 6.2 / 1.2	**24** TU	0007 / 0742 / 1235 / 2005	6.5 / 0.9 / 6.5 / 0.8
10 TU	0018 / 0738 / 1245 / 1958	6.0 / 1.1 / 6.1 / 1.2	**25** W	0059 / 0836 / 1320 / 2057	6.4 / 0.9 / 6.4 / 0.8
11 W	0046 / 0813 / 1316 / 2034	6.0 / 1.2 / 6.1 / 1.3	**26** TH	0148 / 0927 / 1404 / 2148	6.3 / 1.0 / 6.2 / 0.9
12 TH	0120 / 0849 / 1351 / 2111	5.9 / 1.2 / 6.0 / 1.4	**27** F	0236 / 1014 / 1449 / 2237	6.1 / 1.2 / 6.2 / 1.1
13 F	0201 / 0925 / 1433 / 2150	5.7 / 1.3 / 5.8 / 1.5	**28** SA	0325 / 1101 / 1539 / 2326	5.8 / 1.5 / 6.0 / 1.3
14 SA	0251 / 1004 / 1524 / 2235	5.6 / 1.4 / 5.7 / 1.6	**29** SU	0419 / 1147 / 1634	5.6 / 1.7 / 5.8
15 SU	0355 / 1052 / 1626 / 2329	5.5 / 1.8 / 5.7 / 1.7	**30** M	0017 / 0522 / 1236 / 1739	1.6 / 5.5 / 1.9 / 5.7

JULY

	TIME	M		TIME	M
1 TU	0114 / 0631 / 1333 / 1849	1.8 / 5.4 / 2.1 / 5.6	**16** W	0522 / 1210 / 1747	5.6 / 1.9 / 5.8
2 W	0220 / 0735 / 1437 / 1954	1.9 / 5.4 / 2.1 / 5.7	**17** TH	0055 / 0627 / 1324 / 1853	1.7 / 5.6 / 2.0 / 5.8
3 TH	0321 / 0832 / 1536 / 2049	1.9 / 5.6 / 2.0 / 5.7	**18** F	0209 / 0735 / 1443 / 2002	1.7 / 5.6 / 1.9 / 5.8
4 F	0409 / 0922 / 1623 / 2138	1.8 / 5.7 / 1.8 / 5.8	**19** SA	0322 / 0847 / 1559 / 2110	1.6 / 5.8 / 1.6 / 6.0
5 SA	0449 / 1006 / 1704 / 2221	1.6 / 5.9 / 1.6 / 5.9	**20** SU	0435 / 0953 / 1709 / 2214	1.4 / 6.1 / 1.3 / 6.2
6 SU	0527 / 1045 / 1744 / 2259	1.5 / 6.1 / 1.4 / 6.0	**21** M	0544 / 1049 / 1812 / 2311	1.2 / 6.3 / 1.1 / 6.4
7 M	0607 / 1122 / 1827 / 2332	1.3 / 6.2 / 1.3 / 6.0	**22** TU	0649 / 1136 / 1912	1.0 / 6.5 / 0.8
8 TU	0646 / 1154 / 1906	1.2 / 6.3 / 1.2	**23** W	0000 / 0745 / 1219 / 2004	6.5 / 0.9 / 6.6 / 0.7
9 W	0001 / 0724 / 1225 / 1945	6.1 / 1.2 / 6.3 / 1.1	**24** TH	0046 / 0833 / 1300 / 2050	6.5 / 0.8 / 6.6 / 0.6
10 TH	0032 / 0801 / 1259 / 2020	6.1 / 1.2 / 6.3 / 1.2	**25** F	0127 / 0914 / 1340 / 2132	6.4 / 0.9 / 6.6 / 0.8
11 F	0109 / 0832 / 1335 / 2054	6.1 / 1.3 / 6.2 / 1.2	**26** SA	0208 / 0949 / 1420 / 2209	6.2 / 1.0 / 6.4 / 1.0
12 SA	0148 / 0904 / 1413 / 2129	6.0 / 1.3 / 6.2 / 1.2	**27** SU	0250 / 1020 / 1504 / 2244	6.0 / 1.4 / 6.3 / 1.3
13 SU	0232 / 0941 / 1457 / 2209	5.9 / 1.5 / 6.1 / 1.3	**28** M	0336 / 1049 / 1552 / 2319	5.8 / 1.8 / 6.0 / 1.7
14 M	0322 / 1021 / 1548 / 2254	5.8 / 1.6 / 6.0 / 1.5	**29** TU	0428 / 1123 / 1647	5.5 / 2.0 / 5.7
15 TU	0420 / 1109 / 1645 / 2347	5.7 / 1.8 / 5.9 / 1.6	**30** W	0000 / 0534 / 1211 / 1757	2.0 / 5.3 / 2.3 / 5.4
			31 TH	0056 / 0655 / 1316 / 1919	2.2 / 5.2 / 2.4 / 5.3

AUGUST

	TIME	M		TIME	M
1 F	0213 / 0805 / 1444 / 2026	2.3 / 5.3 / 2.4 / 5.4	**16** SA	0149 / 0726 / 1432 / 2002	2.0 / 5.4 / 2.0 / 5.5
2 SA	0328 / 0901 / 1552 / 2121	2.2 / 5.5 / 2.1 / 5.5	**17** SU	0319 / 0857 / 1559 / 2124	1.8 / 5.7 / 1.7 / 5.9
3 SU	0420 / 0946 / 1642 / 2204	1.9 / 5.8 / 1.7 / 5.8	**18** M	0438 / 0956 / 1709 / 2220	1.5 / 6.0 / 1.3 / 6.2
4 M	0505 / 1024 / 1727 / 2238	1.6 / 6.0 / 1.4 / 5.9	**19** TU	0549 / 1042 / 1812 / 2306	1.2 / 6.4 / 0.9 / 6.4
5 TU	0550 / 1057 / 1811 / 2306	1.4 / 6.2 / 1.2 / 6.0	**20** W	0648 / 1122 / 1906 / 2346	0.9 / 6.6 / 0.7 / 6.5
6 W	0632 / 1127 / 1853 / 2336	1.2 / 6.4 / 1.1 / 6.2	**21** TH	0735 / 1158 / 1952	0.8 / 6.7 / 0.6
7 TH	0712 / 1200 / 1931	1.2 / 6.5 / 1.0	**22** F	0022 / 0815 / 1235 / 2030	6.6 / 0.8 / 6.8 / 0.6
8 F	0010 / 0745 / 1234 / 2004	6.3 / 1.1 / 6.5 / 1.0	**23** SA	0059 / 0846 / 1312 / 2103	6.5 / 0.9 / 6.7 / 0.8
9 SA	0046 / 0812 / 1310 / 2033	6.4 / 1.1 / 6.5 / 1.0	**24** SU	0135 / 0910 / 1348 / 2129	6.3 / 1.2 / 6.6 / 1.0
10 SU	0124 / 0840 / 1347 / 2104	6.3 / 1.2 / 6.4 / 1.0	**25** M	0212 / 0929 / 1426 / 2155	6.1 / 1.4 / 6.4 / 1.4
11 M	0204 / 0914 / 1425 / 2141	6.2 / 1.3 / 6.3 / 1.2	**26** TU	0251 / 0949 / 1505 / 2224	5.9 / 1.7 / 6.0 / 1.7
12 TU	0247 / 0952 / 1508 / 2221	6.0 / 1.5 / 6.1 / 1.4	**27** W	0336 / 1020 / 1550 / 2302	5.5 / 2.0 / 5.6 / 2.1
13 W	0339 / 1037 / 1604 / 2313	5.8 / 1.7 / 5.9 / 1.7	**28** TH	0433 / 1118 / 1654 / 2354	5.2 / 2.4 / 5.1 / 2.4
14 TH	0441 / 1134 / 1711	5.6 / 2.0 / 5.6	**29** F	0605 / 1219 / 1842	4.9 / 2.6 / 4.9
15 F	0022 / 0556 / 1257 / 1831	1.9 / 5.4 / 2.2 / 5.4	**30** SA	0107 / 0734 / 1351 / 2005	2.6 / 5.0 / 2.6 / 5.0
			31 SU	0244 / 0834 / 1521 / 2101	2.4 / 5.3 / 2.3 / 5.3

Fig. 7.2   Standard port of Dover (Almanac extract)

RAMSGATE　10-3-14
Kent

CHARTS
Admiralty 1827, 1828; Stanford 5, 19; Imray C1, C8;
OS 179
TIDES
+ 0020 Dover; ML 2.6; Duration 0530; Zone 0 (GMT).
Standard Port DOVER (◄──)

Times				Height (metres)			
HW		LW		MHWS	MHWN	MLWN	MLWS
0000	0600	0100	0700	6.7	5.3	2.0	0.8
1200	1800	1300	1900				

Differences RAMSGATE

+ 0020	+ 0020	− 0007	− 0007	− 1.8	− 1.5	− 0.8	− 0.4

HW Broadstairs = HW Dover + 0040

SHELTER
Good in inner harbour (marina). Access HW − 2 to
HW + 1.
NAVIGATION
Waypoint 51°19'.50N 01°26'.00E, 090°/270° from/to new
breakwater entrance, 0.25M. Beware Dyke Bank to the N,
and Brake and Cross Ledge to the S; all these dry. Only
access is by main channel from the E. Proceed with care
and contact Harbour Control VHF Ch 16 14. Reception
pontoon in West Gully of Royal Harbour.

Fig. 7.3　Ramsgate (Almanac extract)

'Duration' is short for duration of mean rise. This is the average time taken for the tide to rise from any low water level to the next successive high water level.

Time zones

The zone number gives the local standard time difference, if any, from Greenwhich mean time. All times in the almanac are in standard time so that local summer time changes need to be taken into account, as we shall see later.

After the name of the standard port to be used, an arrow indicates the direction to look in the almanac to find its data.

Difference constants

The table between the two lines gives the difference constants to be applied to the standard port data in order to correct that data to the secondary port. The differences often change between spring and neap tides and also with the time of high water. For this reason two sets of data are given for times twelve hours apart and for the extremes of range of mean high water and mean low water at both spring and neap tides.

Using the constants

The difference shown under each condition can be applied directly, if the times and heights on the day you are interested in are close to those given. If not, you will need to choose a value between the two extremes.

For an example, let's look at Ramsgate on 20th June 1986. High water Dover is at 08.57 at a height of 6.1 metres and again at 21.18 with a height of 6.3 metres. These times are about halfway between the times given for Ramgate. We have already said that the tide on the 24th is a spring tide and that the previous neap tide was on the 15th, so our day is about halfway between springs and neaps. Looking at the differences given, you will see that the times of high and low water make no difference to the corrections. You just add 20 minutes for high water and subtract 7 minutes for low water to or from the Dover figures.

There are differences between the spring and neap corrections, however. Mean high water springs gives −1.8 metres whilst mean high water neaps gives −1.5 metres. Use a correction of −1.65 metres in this case. Applying the same method to the low water figures gives a correction of −0.6 metres. Look at Figure 7.4.

It is a good idea to write out a little table like this because not only are you less likely to make mistakes, but if you do, it is much easier to spot them. Later, in Chapter 11, you will meet a special form that can be used for these corrections.

	LW	Ht	HW	Ht
Dover	03.48	1.21	08.57	6.09
Correction	−0.07	−0.60	+0.20	−1.65
Ramsgate	03.41	0.61	09.17	4.44
Dover	16.14	1.38	21.18	6.34
Correction	−0.07	−0.60	+0.20	−1.65
Ramsgate	16.07	0.78	21.38	4.69

Fig. 7.4   Secondary port corrections for Ramsgate, 20th June (Admiralty Tide Tables)

How accurate?

Now we have the times and heights of high and low water at Ramsgate on the day in which we are interested. Two more things need to be remembered. First, we have *calculated* the times to the nearest minute and the heights to the nearest centimetre! Do not fall into the trap of thinking that *prediction* is that accurate. The second thing is that we have not taken into account any of the things we could not predict. Look back to page 72 and see what they were. The idea is to work as accurately as you can with the information given and then treat the results with caution.

British summer time

So far we know the high and low water heights and times, but suppose we expect to arrive some time after 16.00 hours and want to know if we can get in. First we have been working in GMT and, on the 20th June, our clock will be on British Summer Time. This is an hour ahead of GMT so we must add an hour to the calculated times to find the situation at clock time. Some people like to keep the ship's clock at GMT but I find this a nuisance unless I am travelling long distances involving changes of time zone.

Intermediate times

If our boat needs at least 1.5 metres in order not to touch, we are obviously not going to get in at 16.30 BST. The tide is still falling until 17.07 BST We could, of course, make a reasonable guess as to the probable time, but going 'by guess and by God' is not the professional way. Fortunately there is a better way. The Hydrographic Department have been making careful measurements of what happens *between* high and low water at all standard ports over many years and this information is produced in graph form, in the almanac. Figure 7.5 shows the graph for Dover.

Although the information is only produced for the standard ports, the graph of the appropriate standard port, suitably adjusted, can usually be used to find what is happening at a secondary port. The *appropriate* standard port is the one given in the tides sub-section we happen to be using. It may not be the nearest port.

Using the standard port graphs

To use the graph, *in soft pencil*, first enter the *time* of high water after our expected arrival time at Ramsgate (from Figure 7.4) in the box, bottom centre, on the graph. Now complete the times in all the other boxes. Next, look at the grid to the left of the graph and mark, on the top line, the point corresponding to the *height* of that high water at Ramsgate. Do the same on the bottom line for the height of low water before it. Join these two points with a light pencil line.

In our example we want 1.5 metres for the boat and, let us say, an extra metre for safety so: on the same HW and LW height lines, mark the 2.5 metre points and join them with a second light pencil line. Now put your straight edge on the point where your two pencil lines cross, and draw a third line parallel to the top line to cut all the curved graph lines. We are half way between spring and neap tides, so put the straight edge on a point on the line you have just drawn, halfway between where it cuts the spring (continuous) and neap (dotted) graph lines on the left. Now draw a line vertically down. This line will cut the time line at the earliest time *before* high water when the depth will be 2.5 metres. You should have made it about 18.55. Remember this time is still GMT. Add 1 hour to make it BST.

Working the other way

If you know the time but not the height, you could still draw the same last three lines starting from the known point on the time line. If you were expecting to leave the port a few hours later, a line drawn from where your horizontal line cuts the right hand curve, down to the time line, will give you the last time *after* high water that you could safely depart.

Figure 7.5 is reproduced in Appendix A with all the lines drawn in. I have put arrows on the lines to show the sequence in which they were drawn. If you did not get the same answer as me, you can use it to check. Once you have made a check on your work and recorded the result, it is best to rub out the pencil lines and times so that they will not cause confusion next time.

If you have managed so far, you have completed what most people find to be one of the most difficult parts of navigation classes. If you have not succeeded, don't despair. Work slowly through again and see if you can spot your error. Try a few more of your own for practice. I have put a couple more examples in Appendix A, with answers, but do try to work them through first before you look at these answers.

Rule of twelfths

With the introduction of the graphical method of calculation in 1986, the rule of twelfths has less importance than hitherto. It is still a useful quick method of calculation however, and I still think many people will use it.

The method is based on the mathematical sine wave but fortunately that need not concern you. All you need to do is look at the curve given in the tide tables for the port you are interested in. If that curve is a smooth one with both sides more or less even, the rule will work. If it looks reasonab. , work out the range between high and low water and divide by twelve.

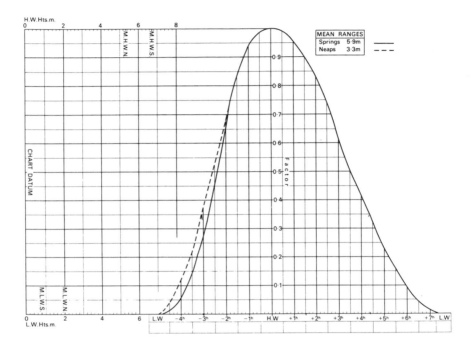

Fig. 7.5   Dover mean Spring and Neap curves

Taking the first tide at Ramsgate from Figure 7.4, we find low water is 0.61 and high water 4.44, subtracting one from the other gives 3.83, which is the range. One twelfth of this is 0.32 (approx.).

The rule says that the rise and fall of the tide is as follows: 1st hour 1/12th, 2nd hour 2/12ths, 3rd hour 3/12ths, 4th hour 3/12ths, 5th hour 2/12ths, and 6th hour 1/12th.

This would mean that at, say, two hours after low water the tide will have risen by 1/12th in the first hour and 2/12ths in the second, making 3/12ths in all, i.e. 0.96 metres. This, added to the low water figure of 0.61, would give a height above charted figures of 1.57 metres. For practice, try doing it the other way, using the graph, and see what difference you get.

Unless you are prepared to enter a harbour on the basis that a few centimetres of clearance is enough, the differences you get are too small to matter. Remember, it only works when the graph is a smooth one (actually sinusoidal), so allow a good margin for error if you use the method.

8

Tides: Ebb and Flow

⚓

What you will learn

How the tide causes the surface of the sea to move.
   How these movements can be predicted and where the predictions are recorded.
   How the movements affect a vessel at sea.
   The meanings and effects of tidal set and leeway.

By the time you have completed the chapter you will know

What a tidal set is and how to find its value at a particular place and time.
   How the tidal set is related to boat movement.
   How to calculate a boat's absolute movement taking into account tidal set and movement over the surface of the sea.
   How to allow for leeway.
   How to find a vessel's course and/or position after taking the above factors into account.

What you will need

A soft (2B) pencil and a ruler or straight edge.
   A pair of dividers and a protractor (or suitable substitutes).
   Preferably but not essentially, the Nautical Almanac you used in Chapter 6.

Now that we have got past the ups and downs of tides, it is time to look at what happens to all that water as it moves in other directions. A lot of the ideas that were explained in Chapter 7 will be applied here.

Sources of information

Because of all the variables involved, *calculation* of the stream at any particular place is extremely difficult. It is also unnecessary because it is actually easier to *measure* it. This, the Hydrographic Office have been doing for many years. Because they have collected so much data, the mean values are pretty accurate.

Tidal atlas

Tidal information is published in two ways. Both ways, although they use the same information, are quite differently presented. The first is a series of booklets called Tidal Atlases. Each booklet covers an area of sea, the actual size of the area depending on both how complicated the stream is and also how busy the area. A separate booklet covers the Channel Islands for example, because the tides there are both strong and complex. Figure 8.1 shows a page from this booklet.

There are actually 12 pages like Figure 8.1 in each booklet; one for each hour. Copies of the chartlets usually appear in almanacs. Often these are very much reduced in size and are lacking the latitude and longitude scales. This makes them more difficult to use than the Admiralty Tidal Atlases.

In order to use the booklet it is best to note in pencil, at the top of each page, the times in relation to high water at the reference port. Start this on the page headed high water. Notice that the high water referred to is HW Dover. This is the reference port for most UK waters. Remember the relation to high water Dover given in the tidal correction data for Ramsgate in Chapter 7? If the note is in soft pencil it can easily be rubbed out when no longer required.

If you try to enter more than two high waters at a time, you are liable to confuse yourself. Before you start, clean off any old figures. Having entered the times of high water on the proper page, work forward and backward through the book adding or subtracting an hour for each successive page. At the end, check that you have not made a mistake. You can do this by making sure that the time for six hours before high water is within about a half to one hour of that for six hours after high water.

Using the atlas

Using the atlas is easy, once the times have been entered. All you need to do is find your present position on the page nearest to the actual

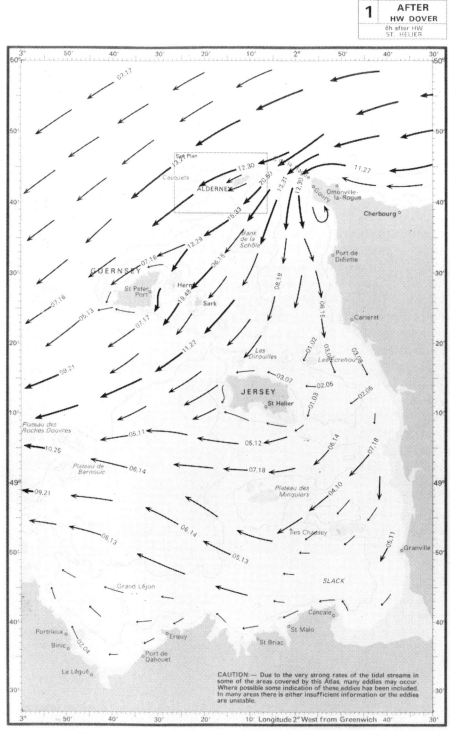

Fig. 8.1 Example of a Tidal Atlas page (Booklet NP 264)

time now, or a future position at the time you expect to arrive there. Then look at the arrow which is nearest to that position. Two pieces of information are available. The direction in which the arrow is drawn gives the direction of the stream or SET, and the figures beside it the rate of the stream. If no figures are given beside the arrow, all is not lost. The arrows vary in both thickness and length. The relative *sizes* of the arrows indicate the strength of the stream, so the figures on any arrow nearby, of the same size as the arrow you are using which does have figures, can be used.

Reading the rates

The figures are in pairs separated by a comma, not a decimal point. The two digits before the comma are the mean neap rate and the two after it, the mean spring rate. It is important to realise that *the figures shown are in tenths of a knot*. For example, 12,30 would be read as mean neap rate 1.2 knots, and mean spring rate 3.0 knots. A tide of either 12 or 30 knots would be very improbable, even in the Channel Isles. In some areas this is not so obvious.

If, on the day you want, the tide is somewhere between springs and neaps, then you must take an in-between value. On June 20th 1986, the date used in Chapter 7, the tide is halfway between springs and neaps, so the value to use in the example above would be 2.1 knots. If high water Dover is above the mean spring rate, take the higher value, i.e. 3.0 knots; do not extrapolate.

Tidal diamonds

Tidal diamonds are part of the second method by which tidal data is provided. Scattered over any chart you will see a series of these magenta diamond shapes, each with a letter in it. In a convenient position on the chart you will find a table, Figure 8.2 shows an example, listing all the diamonds with data, again for 12 hours. This time the direction is given as a true bearing and the stream is given as a set of figures. The figures show values in knots to one place of decimals. It is important to remember that these values are *averages of past tides*. Predictions are not this accurate. The information given for a particular tidal diamond position is quite precise, but it is history.

Often there will be no diamond where you want it to be. Taking an intermediate value for positions between diamonds should only be done with caution. Measurements are only made where the Hydrographer considers it important. This means that they are often

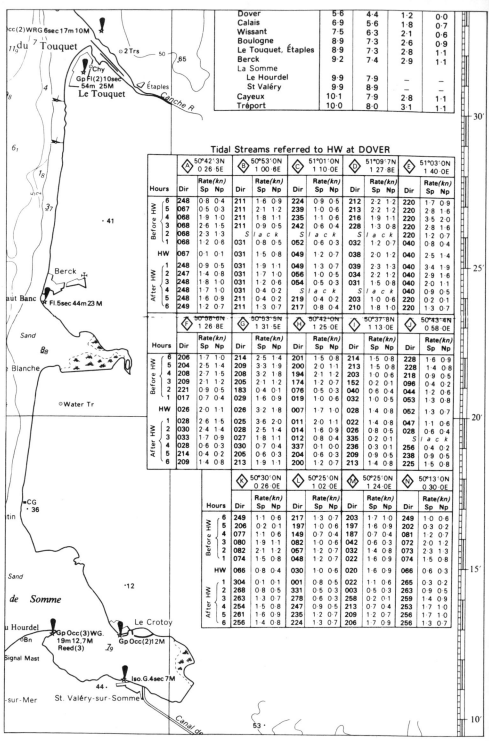

Fig. 8.2 Tidal Diamonds (Chart 5052)

placed where the stream is unusual in some way. It is not certain that the stream halfway between two diamonds will be the mean value. Some experience is needed to get the best results since, in deciding the most likely values, account must be taken of such things as changes in depth and contours.

Tide streams and boat movement

Now we come to the next tricky bit! This often causes the most problems, but this is mainly because many people try to tackle it in mathematical terms. This is a neat, economical and precise way to work – if you are mathematically inclined. If not, the mere mention of calculus, trigonometry or vector geometry can cause strong men to weep. Fear not! Stick with me and I promise not to mention any of them again. I will use the term 'vector', but this is just an easier way of describing a line representing something that has both size and direction.

Let me try to show what actually happens when a boat moves on tidal water, but on a small scale so that you can visualise it. To do that we need a model again, so that we can build a mental picture.

Another model

Imagine a large chess board over which is laid a large sheet of plastic film, so that we can still see the board whilst being able to move the plastic around over it. On top of the plastic sheet is placed a little toy yacht. The chess board is the land, with the squares forming a grid like that on a chart; the plastic is the sea and the toy boat is a yacht. I am going to have wheels on the boat for reasons which will become clear later. Now we can apply forces, one at a time, and slowly, and actually see what happens.

Forces at work

Start by imagining the boat in the position shown at O in Figure 8.3, its bows pointing along one of the grid lines. If I blow gently from behind the boat, it will move, *over* the plastic, along the line from square to square. On stopping the blowing we can see how far the boat has moved by counting the squares. If, instead of blowing, I pull the plastic sheet, the boat will still move over the board but now *with* the plastic in whichever direction I pull it. In Figure 8.3 the boat has now moved from B to P. Since I started it has gone from O through B, to P.

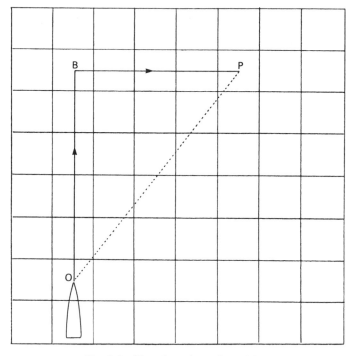

Fig. 8.3 The chess board model

Combining the forces

Let's now put these movements together. I now start blowing *and* pulling at the same time. The boat will now move, both *over and with* the plastic. At sea this is what happens. The forces of wind and tide are both acting at the same time. A boat moves both over and with the sea. As far as the boat on the sea or the boat on the board are concerned, each is moving under the influence of two forces. If those two forces are in different directions, the boat will move in two directions at once. If they are in either the same or opposite directions, the boat will move either faster, or more slowly. It is the combined effect of these two forces, called the resultant, that we are interested in.

If you think about the actual movement, or even try it, you will realise that the boat did not move along the lines from O to B and then from B to P. Both movements actually took place at the same time so that the *real* movement was in a straight line from O to P. I have drawn in that movement as a broken line on Figure 8.3. This is the actual path taken by the boat, provided that both the blowing and pulling movements were done at constant rates. The RESULTANT of the two forces will be a movement along the dotted line of Figure 8.3, directly from O to P. If either rate changes during the movement, then the dotted line will not be straight.

Relative motion

This actual path is the relative motion of the boat over the board. At sea, this is often called the GROUND TRACK or COURSE AND DISTANCE MADE GOOD, because it represents the direction, and distance, that the boat travels over the sea bed. We can now apply the model situation to the real 'yacht-at-sea' situation. It is important to remember that we plotted, on the paper, how far each force had moved the toy boat in the same period of time. In practice it is easier to use the term 'rate', and draw the lines in knots, which are sea miles per hour. These lines are vectors. On each, the size represents the rate and the direction, or bearing. All the lines must be drawn to the same scale, otherwise it has the effect of changing the rates.

The movement resulting from blowing is the sailing movement. That is, the rate at which the boat moves over the water. The amount of movement in a given time can be found from the log, if the log reading and time are recorded regularly. The pulling movement represents the tide stream. This can be found from the tidal atlas or from tidal diamonds.

Leeway

Before progressing, let's go back to the chess board model and look at what happens if, instead of blowing from behind the boat, the sails are set and the blowing comes from one side. With no movement of the plastic at all, we find that the toy boat no longer moves along the line in which its wheels are pointed. The wheels slip a bit on the plastic and, although it still moves forward, its path is now at a small angle to the original line.

This is exactly what happens to a yacht at sea. If the wind is coming from anywhere other than behind a yacht, it still moves forwards, but at the same time it slips sideways a little, away from the wind. This is LEEWAY, and is recorded as an angle from the line along which the boat is pointing (the ship's heading) on the side away from the wind. If this is included in the diagram, the drawing looks like Figure 8.4. The position, marked P, which takes into account tide and leeway as well as the log and course steered, is called an estimated position. More is said about this in Chapter 9.

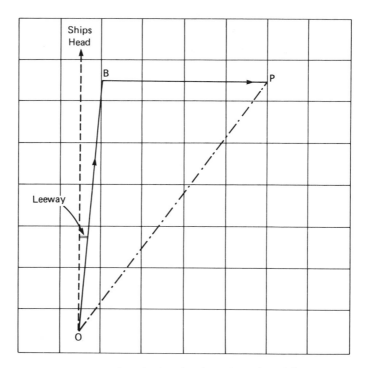

Fig. 8.4   Developing the chess board model

Allowing for leeway

No confusion need arise as to what to do with leeway if you picture what is happening. If the wind is coming from the port side of the boat, as in Figure 8.4, it will have the effect of turning the water track away from the ship's heading in a clockwise direction. Since bearings increase in a clockwise direction, leeway must, on port tack, be added to the ship's heading to get the water track. If the wind is on the starboard side, the reverse is true, so leeway must then be subtracted.

Drawing the movements

Now, to make sure that you have followed what has been covered, take a sheet of squared or graph paper and draw the directions and movements which will result from the example below. You will need first to:

1   Choose a scale. If your paper is about A4 size, 1 centimetre or 0.5 inches per knot will do nicely.

2   Mark the start point with the letter O near the bottom, about four squares from the left hand corner.

3   Mark the top, bottom, right and left edges of your paper N, S, E and W respectively.

4   Find a pencil and ruler!

Don't worry about a protractor; just estimate the angles for the moment.

Example 8.1

In the first hour a boat sails north at a steady three knots, with the wind and tide behind it. The tide is running at one knot. The boat turns East for a while and his speed increases to four knots. After half an hour the wind goes round to the North East and the boat goes back onto a northerly course. The tide is unchanged. The boat stays on this course for two hours and then turns west to enter harbour. This takes one hour. How far is the boat from the start when it reaches the harbour entrance? Did you think I was going to ask the name of the skipper?

I have done this one, and the answer is in Appendix A (pages 164–5). Have a go at this but don't look at the answer yet. Try the next example first (on page 98), and *then* look.

Cumulative effects

A few moments' study of the tidal atlas, or the tidal diamond data, will show you that the tide is not constant with time. Boat speed is not likely to be exactly constant either. This need not actually cause a problem when we plot the diagram. You can deal with the changes in two ways.

In the first method, you add up, or read from, the log, the *total* distance sailed in the *total* time and, using the *average* course steered, draw that line on the chart. Then plot all the different tide movements over the time period, joining them one on another from the end of the first line as in Figure 8.5. You can really only do this if there is no real change in the course.

The other way is to draw a separate sailed line for *each hour* and then join to it a separate line for *each hour's tide change*. Figure 8.6 shows this method. In the chess board model used earlier, this was being done automatically and we found the real path of the boat by modelling it. When we do the job on paper this is not possible, at least not without special mathematical techniques.

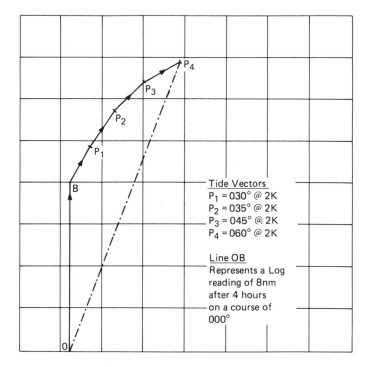

Tide Vectors
$P_1 = 030° @ 2K$
$P_2 = 035° @ 2K$
$P_3 = 045° @ 2K$
$P_4 = 060° @ 2K$

Line OB
Represents a Log
reading of 8nm
after 4 hours
on a course of
000°

Fig. 8.5 Allowing for tide: Method 1

Accuracy

There are some important differences between the two drawing
methods used, although both end up at the same place. The first
method is neater, since it means far fewer pencil lines on the chart, but
notice that it produces a track line which is straight. Line up a straight
edge with the track line produced by the second method and you will
find that the track line is not straight. Which is correct?

Course made good

The answer to this question is actually neither, but the second method
is more correct than the first! Both methods are used and both work. A
little thought will tell you when not to use the first method. For
instance, if part of your route is over shallow or dangerous waters, you
will need to know more precisely where you are actually going. In
rocky coastal waters, hourly plots would be much better. If you are on
the open sea, however, you might do plots at six hourly, or even twelve
hourly intervals safely. Remember that a completely accurate ground

track line will represent your COURSE MADE GOOD over the ground. That course must be possible *without hitting anything*.

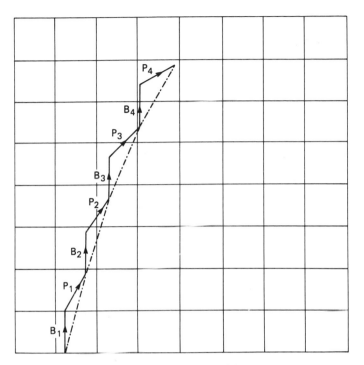

Fig. 8.6 Allowing for tide: Method 2

Order of drawing

You may have noticed that, in every case, I have drawn the water track line first. It does not actually matter which you draw first, provided that both tide and course vectors are drawn with the arrows going in the same direction, away from the starting point.

Names of vectors

Each of the vectors drawn has a name which describes it and which is conventionally used. They are all illustrated in Figure 8.7.

The first line drawn is simply the ship's heading and this is not actually a vector since it is a direction only. It is needed in order to draw the next line which makes allowance for leeway. This line is called the WATER TRACK, because it shows the direction and distance the boat moves over the water. The next line is the TIDAL VECTOR, which represents the movement over the sea bed resulting *only* from the tide. Combining the water track with the tidal vector gives the ground track, which is called the COURSE MADE GOOD, because it represents what the boat actually does.

I now need to point out a few things which may not have been obvious as you studied the first part of this chapter.

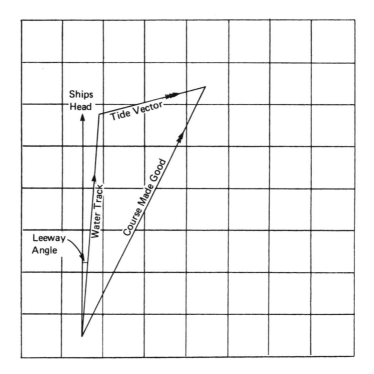

Fig. 8.7   Naming the vectors

Course to steer

The diagrams all finished up with three vectors: the water track, the tidal vector and the course and distance made good. The latter was the one found from the other two. This will not be true every time you draw a vector diagram. Sometimes, when planning a journey, you will know the course that must be made good, perhaps it's through a narrow channel, or one that will get you from one place to another. What you want to know is the course to *steer*. This can be found by drawing on the chart the course you *wish* to make good and then setting off against it the tidal vectors that you anticipate will affect that course. Figure 8.8 gives an example.

Notice that the same rules have been applied. The same two vectors have been drawn head-to-tail going away from the start point. Finding an estimated position, and finding a course to steer, are two completely different operations and must not be confused. Remember that, in our example, we have started with the direction of the course *to be* made good; the resultant is known. This is only half a vector though, because we do not know the rate and so cannot mark on it the distance. It is actually the direction of the water track that you need to know. The problem is that, until the journey is complete, you do not know how long it takes. You can get round this problem by using what you do know, and informed guesses based on what you know.

Start by drawing in and measuring the length of the line we wish to follow, the course made good. Next make an estimate of how long this is likely to take based on a reasonable average speed. Then calculate the tide effect during that period. These are the things that you know or can estimate fairly accurately. Two approaches to the problem are now available.

Short passages

If the passage time is relatively short, say under about two hours, the tide vector direction will probably not change appreciably over the period. If it does, what follows must be done in separate stages for each change.

Construction

We can calculate the direction and the rate, sometimes called the DRIFT, of this vector and draw it on the chart, going away from the starting point of the passage. It is usual, but not essential, to use one hour of tide. The point is that it is only going to be used for constructing the vector diagram. It needs to be long enough for accurate drawing and no more. So long as the vectors are all drawn to the *same* scale, it does not matter what that scale is.

Look at Figure 8.8 and see what I have done. Take the dividers and set them to the distance that would be covered, at the estimated speed chosen, during the same period as the tidal vector period. We are using a speed of five knots and have drawn a tidal vector for three hours, since the stream is constant over this period. The dividers should be set at 15 miles so that the same period of time is used.

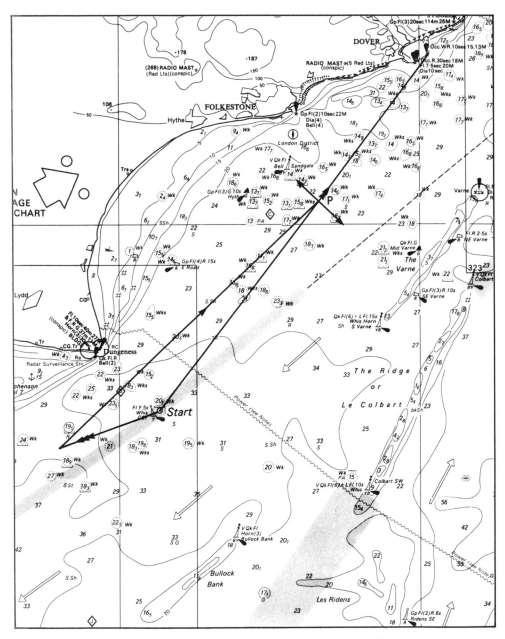

Fig. 8.8   Finding a course to steer (Chart 5052)

One point of the dividers is now placed on the end of the tidal vector and the other swung until it meets the course line drawn earlier. That point is then marked. I have drawn an arc crossing the course line in Figure 8.8 (point P) so that you can see what I mean. Joining these two points then gives the water track line. Its length we know, and its direction, which is what we want to know, can now be measured.

If I maintain a speed of five knots for three hours, I should then be at point P. I can check progress as I go and, if it is working, I could do the same thing again at P for the new tide conditions.

How fast am I going over the ground? If I divide OP by three this will tell me. If I reach P in three hours, how long before I get past Folkestone Pier, if the tide stays the same? The distance until Folkestone Pier is abeam, is about three miles from P on this course. I am only doing 3.3 knots over the ground, so it will take me about 55 minutes if the tide stays the same.

Work this through yourself and see how I get my answers. It will help you in the next chapter.

Caution

A common mistake made with this method is to draw the tide vector and then join it to the destination. This will give a totally wrong answer unless the passage actually takes exactly the same time as that allowed for the tidal vector. Remember all vectors in a diagram must be drawn to the same scale!

Speed over the ground

The distance OP represents the distance travelled in the time interval chosen. If one hour had been used for construction, this distance would actually represent the speed over the ground in knots. To find the total passage time, we simply divide the total distance by this speed. One hour would have resulted in a very small, and therefore inaccurate, construction on this chart.

The impact of leeway

Leeway must be applied to the water track bearing in order to arrive at the COURSE TO STEER. Because we are now going from water track to ship's heading, the leeway correction will be the reverse of what we did before. The water track is always away from the ship's heading on the down wind side. In the first example, I have made no allowance for leeway.

A further example will help to make this clear. You do not need to use a chart, the same piece of graph paper will do, but this time you will need a protractor. Use the same scale and a starting point position four squares to the East of that in the last example.

Example 8.2

A boat sails North East at a steady three knots for three hours with the wind and tide behind it. The tide is running at one knot. The boat then turns North West for two hours and its speed increases to five knots. There is now ten degrees of leeway. The wind then goes round to the West and decreases. The boat goes back onto a northerly course still with ten degrees of leeway, but now its speed is down to three knots. The boat stays on this course for two more hours. For the first hour the tide is slack and then runs at two knots from North East for the next hour. During these two hours, leeway is still ten degrees. How far has the boat travelled over the ground from the start?

The answer is in Appendix A, with the answer to Example 8.1. Before you look, try plotting the passage.

Longer passages

If the passage is a much longer one, you may find that the tide changes direction markedly over the period. In this case it is best to plot all the tidal vectors from the start for the whole of the estimated time of the journey.

A worked example

You need not actually do this on the chart. You can use graph paper provided that you maintain the scale. You can then transfer the resultant, which will be the direction and distance between the two ends to the chart. This resultant is the net total displacement over the period. If you then join the end of this to the destination, it will give you a course to steer after allowing for leeway. Figure 8.9 shows an imaginary passage from Appleport to Pomme using this method. I have actually plotted the tidal vectors on the chart so that you can see them.

This method is a great deal easier to do and involves far less chartwork than you would need if you worked each hour separately. It is important to realise that you will not actually sail down *any* of the lines you have drawn. The boat's probable ground track is shown as a dotted line in Figure 8.9. The other thing to remember is that the accuracy of the course depends not only on the accuracy of your plotting but also on how good your estimate of the passage time was:

Advantage of separate plot

If, for some reason, you change your plan part way through the passage, it is a simple matter to transfer that part of the tidal vector already covered, to the chart. A revised plan can then be started from this information. This method will be mentioned again in Chapter 10 when we look at passage planning.

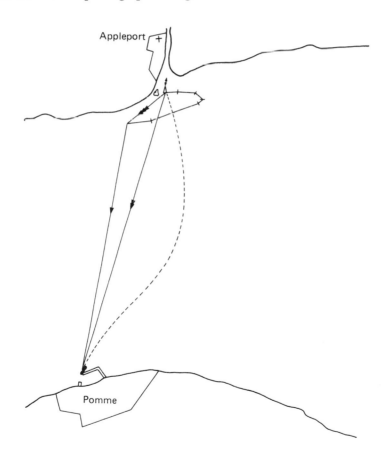

Fig. 8.9 Tide vectors on a longer passage

Arrow convention

You will have noticed that on Figures 8.8 and 8.9 I have put a different number of arrows onto each vector. Although it is not crucial, this is the convention normally used and, if it is observed, it helps when looking at someone else's plotting. One arrow head is used for the water track, two for the ground track (course made good) and three for the tidal vector.

Reflections

This chapter may have been hard going but, together with Chapter 7, it has covered all the tidal work you need to understand to be able to navigate. In the next chapter we shall start to put it all into practice.

9

Chartwork

_____ ⚓ _____

What you will learn

How to obtain position lines and use them to find your position at sea.
   The methods of position fixing available to you.
   How to record a position once found.
   How to estimate a position after allowing for variables.
   How to make provision for compass variation and deviation.
   When and how to make the records needed to keep track of your progress.

By the time you have completed the chapter you will know

How to use the various fixing methods to find your position.
   How to find your position in relation to an earlier known position.
   How to keep track of your progress on a passage.

What you will need

The drawing instruments and pencils already used earlier.
   A chart for practice would be useful but is not essential.

The information available from charts has been dealt with in Chapter 6, whilst the last two chapters have looked at the way the tide causes the boat to move in relation to the land. Now we shall put all this together and see how it is possible to mark a precise spot on the chart and say: 'That is where I am!'.

Position finding

In the sort of sailing done by most people there are two ways used to find out one's position. You can start from a known point and keep a check on all your movements both as to distance and to direction. This is called DEAD RECKONING, and was the method mentioned in Chapter 8. Or you can find your position from time to time in relation to fixed objects that you can see. Such a position is called a FIX. In practice, you will usually use a mixture of both methods on most passages.

Position Fixing

I shall start with *obtaining a fix* because this is actually how we all start when going to sea for the first time. The boat sails out of the harbour and, even as a passenger, one looks at a radio mast on the shore, the breakwater or perhaps a recognisable headland. From these sightings one can say to oneself: 'We are about five miles from Folkestone'. What you are actually doing is making a series of estimates of distance and direction, and combining the results to decide where you are.

When you are *navigating* the boat, more accurate means have to be employed. This is where the hand-bearing compass comes in. Instead of guessing, you use the compass to *measure* the bearings to the mast, the breakwater and the headland. The bearings you measure are *magnetic* bearings and must be converted into *true* bearings by applying *variation*, as was described in Chapter 6, before they can be drawn on the chart.

Now look at Figure 9.1. Each bearing measured can be drawn on the chart as a line passing through the object used. In order to have obtained that *particular* value, the boat must have been on that line *somewhere* at the moment the bearing was measured. This is called a POSITION LINE. If all three bearings have been taken in a very short space of time, the boat will not have moved far.

Three point fix

Since the boat had to be on *every* position line when the bearings were taken, the only place it could have been is where they all cross. This is called a THREE POINT FIX, because three fixed points on shore have been used to obtain it. Of course, in real life, they will not cross at *exactly* the same spot. Inaccuracy of measurement and of drawing, as well as the impossibility of measuring them all at one precise instant, will see to that.

This is the reason for using three points. If we took only two and made a bad mistake in reading, converting to true, or drawing, they might still cross, but in completely the wrong place. We might even

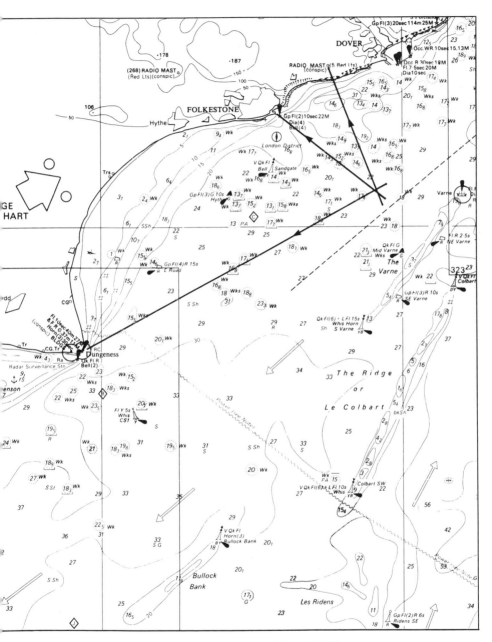

Fig. 9.1 A three point fix (Chart 5052)

have picked the wrong hotel or the wrong church! With three points, these sort of errors usually show up because the position lines do not cross at anywhere near one point. Instead, a small triangle is produced – even a large triangle if you have made a big mistake. This triangle is called a cocked hat. The size of the cocked hat gives an indication of the reliability of the fix.

If you get, as you usually do, a cocked hat you are *probably*, but not *necessarily*, somewhere inside it. Think about that for a moment and you should realise that any error could be to either side of each position line. The thing to do is to assume that you are within the triangle at whatever place is nearest to danger.

Other fixes

To fix a position, one needs position lines. It is not *essential* to have three. Sometimes you will have to make do with only two *identifiable* objects. It is possible to fix your position using only one object, as you will see.

You do not actually have to *see* the objects. As long as you can *detect* them, they can be used. Detection may be by radar or by radio. So long as the detecting apparatus can tell you the direction, you are in business. The use of electronic detection is discussed in Chapter 11. It is best to learn basic navigation techniques before you progress to other means.

Transit lines

It is not always necessary to use a compass to get a position line. You will often find, if you look at the chart or the shore, that certain objects are in line.

When two objects are in line with a third they are said to be in transit. If your boat is the third object, then the line drawn through all three is a very reliable position line. If you have two such lines that cross where you need to be, you can fix your position accurately by observation alone.

Running fix

This is the least accurate method of fixing your position, but it may be the only one available to you on occasion. Imagine you are sailing in bad visibility and you see faintly the glow of a lightship. You can recognise which one it is by its light. You can take a bearing and get a position line but where on that line are you?

What you do is obtain two position lines with a time interval between them. Note the log reading and time when you take each bearing. During that time interval you carefully work out how far and in what direction you have travelled. You can measure how far on your log. The direction will be the ground track direction which was described in Chapter 8. Armed with this information you are ready to start.

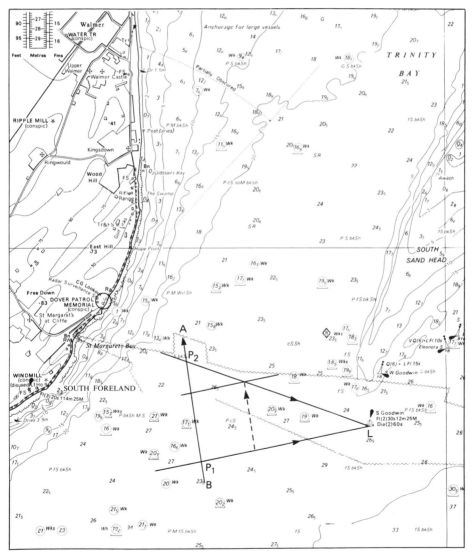

Fig. 9.2 A running fix (Chart 5043)

First you draw in on the chart both position lines passing through the lightship. In Figure 9.2 these are lines LP1 and LP2. Next, draw a line cutting both position lines in the direction of your ground track. This is line AB in Figure 9.2. You know how far you have travelled on the log and you should, by now, have made any correction for tide. With your dividers set to this distance (calculated in the same way as in Chapter 8), put one point on the junction between the first position line LP1 and AB, and mark the point on AB reached by the other end of the dividers. Now draw a line through this point, parallel to the first position line, to cut the second position line. This is the point where you were when the second position line bearing was measured.

Figure 9.2 shows the whole construction. The dotted line is the path of the boat between the two position lines. If you know a little geometry, you will be able to understand how this works, but it is not essential in order to use the method.

Recording fixes

After you have plotted a fix on the chart, it is best to rub out most of the construction lines. If you do not, it can get very messy. You should have a little notebook in which you can jot down which objects were used, the measured bearings and any correcting you did, so that if you need to check later, you can do so.

On the chart, a fix is indicated by a dot in a small circle. Beside it you should write the time and the log reading.

Composite fixes

For some reason, a lot of people regard each fixing method as exclusive. There is no reason why you should not combine any or all of the methods of producing position lines to get a fix. The object of the exercise is to get a reliable idea of where you are.

Position Estimation

The dead reckoning method of position finding relies on three things. Where you started from, how far you have gone and the direction you have been heading. This means that a dead reckoning position, or DR as it is usually called, is not an actual position. It makes no allowance for leeway or for tide. It is useful for keeping track but needs refinement to find out where you actually are.

When the tide and leeway have been taken into account, you arrive at an ESTIMATED POSITION normally abbreviated to EP. On a short coastal passage it is usual to work out a DR position every one or two hours. If this position can be checked using regular fixes, it may not be necessary to work out an EP every time.

Chart plotting

In conditions of poor visibility it is best to work out the EP each time you record the DR. This is because you may not have a fix to check it with. The same is true of any passage off shore when you have nothing to use for a fix.

Rhumb lines

Imagine you are going to make a passage from A to B which involves a sea crossing. You start by using a large scale chart which shows both ends of the journey. This is sometimes called a passage planning chart. On this chart you begin by drawing a line joining the starting point and the destination. This line must be possible to sail! It must not pass over land or through water too shallow to sail in. This line is called a RHUMB line. Some people prefer not to draw the rhumb line in because, they argue, if you do you will try to sail along it. We have said enough now for *you* to understand that it is a construction line only.

Extracting the facts

Once the rhumb line is on the chart you can start gathering and recording information. How far is it? Is it a straight line? If we know the average speed for our boat, how long will it take?

All this information should go into your notebook along with the tidal information for the dates of the passage. You can do it on your dining room table before leaving home. It is really part of passage planning which is discussed in Chapter 10. The diagram, Figure 9.3 and the notes in Figure 9.4, show an example of this kind of preparation.

Getting started

When the trip starts, we sail out of the harbour knowing quite a lot already. Having calculated the course to steer by the method used in Chapter 8, we know the direction we want to go in. We also know what to expect the tide to be doing to us. What we do not know are the

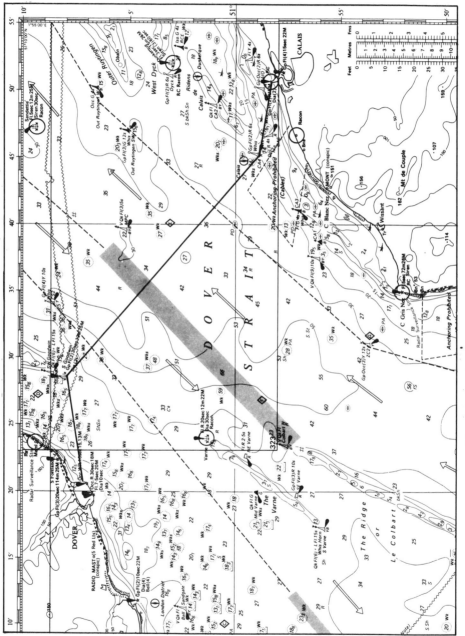

Fig. 9.3   Putting in the rhumb line (Chart 5052)

wind and sea conditions, our actual leeway and speed. We don't know if we can actually steer the course we would like. We shall soon find out.

Passage   DOVER TO CALAIS

Depart   20th June 1986

NOTES:-

1. *Shipping Lanes*. Must cross at right angles.
   ∴ Head for S. Goodwin L.V. and cross from there

2. *Distances and Courses*   Miles   Bearing

	Miles	Bearing
Dover to S. Goodwin	5.0	82°T
S. Goodwin to Calais Nº4 By	13.8	132°T
CA 4 By to Calais	3.2	100°T
TOTAL	22.0	

3. *Times*
     @ 4 K = 5hrs 30 mins @ 6 K 3 hours 40 mins

4. *H.W. Dover*
   08.57 & 21.18 (GMT)   09.57 & 22.18 (BST)

Fig. 9.1   Starting the Plan

Deviation

At this point another problem mentioned in Chapter 6 needs to be considered. This is the problem of deviation. Remember that I said that the compass will have errors caused by magnetic materials in the vessel. When we are talking about the course to steer, we actually mean the TRUE course. When we apply variation to the true course we get the MAGNETIC course. Only after we have made allowance for deviation, do we get the COMPASS course which is the one the helmsperson wants to know about.

So far I have ignored this complication. From now on it will be taken into account. The method is not difficult. The thing to remember is that deviation changes depending on the ship's heading. This means that it is the last thing to make adjustment for when calculating the compass course. Whether we add or subtract depends whether the deviation is East or West. Some people like the mnemonic 'Cadet' meaning compass add East true. I prefer 'error east, compass least; error west, compass best'. This can then apply to both deviation and variation. Remember the order matters. It is:

TRUE⟷VARIATION⟷MAGNETIC⟷DEVIATION⟷COMPASS

Outside the harbour

Once out of the harbour, having made the corrections, we find we can sail the course we want. We find a convenient buoy or take a very careful fix and call this our DEPARTURE POINT (DP). All DR and EP plots that we are going to put on the chart are based on this, so it needs to be as good as possible. At the DP we start the log, either by setting it to zero or making a note of the reading. If it is the trailing type, it will need to be streamed now.

Finding the leeway

If we know the boat very well we will have a pretty good idea of what the leeway is in most situations. If not, we must find out. The leeway is the difference between the *course steered* and the WAKE COURSE, which is the line of disturbed water that appears in all good drawings of boats sailing. The trouble is that most modern boats leave very little wake! Certainly not enough to measure its line.

The way to get over this problem is to find some conspicuous object close in line with the DP and the course steered. Soon after you pass the DP take a bearing on this object. If you then take a further bearing after about a mile, the difference between the two bearings, after allowing for tide, is your leeway. Don't forget to note the time and log reading each time you take a bearing. To allow for tide you will have to draw a vector diagram as in Figure 9.5.

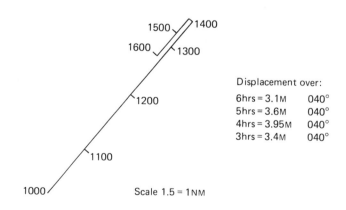

Displacement over:

6hrs = 3.1M	040°
5hrs = 3.6M	040°
4hrs = 3.95M	040°
3hrs = 3.4M	040°

Scale 1.5 = 1NM

Fig. 9.5   What the tide will do

Tacking

If you cannot sail the desired course you will have to tack from side to side of it. The best way to do this is to get to your DP then find what is the *best course you can steer* towards the direction you want.

Having established this, draw it on your chart. You can then either sail this course for a fixed time, *or* for a fixed distance, before tacking again. Each time you tack, a DR position must be recorded and the new course line must be drawn on the chart.

Always wait to settle on the new course before plotting it. In practice it often takes a little time to establish exactly what the best course is. The same information is recorded every time the course is changed. Figure 9.6 shows how this might look after several hours. There is no need to do an EP each time you change course. If you can get the occasional fix, this should be done and plotted. You can see these in Figure 9.6.

Making and marking progress

Before we started we will have decided how often to update our position on the chart. Let's say we have decided that every three hours will do.

Suppose we cannot see

Let's now imagine that visibility is not too good and we are not able to get fixes. Figure 9.7 shows such a situation for the same passage. Each time a change of course is made, it is recorded on the chart until by 12.00 we have been tacking into an East wind every half hour. I have assumed leeway of five degrees and allowed for this when plotting. I could have drawn the course steered lines in, and then set off the leeway but this would have made many more lines on the chart to confuse us.

Getting an EP

At 12.00 we decide we can set off across the shipping lanes. At 13.00 we have a DR position with leeway allowed, but we still cannot see anything. We decide that we need to know better where we are. If we have been careful, all we need to add is the tide. Looking at the tidal plot in our notes (Figure 9.5) we find that the total tide for the three hours just gone is 3.5 miles in a direction 040 degrees. This is plotted

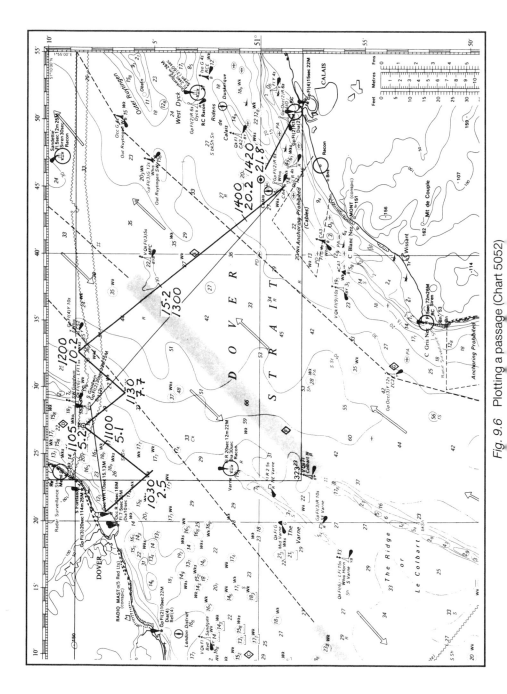

Fig. 9.6 Plotting a passage (Chart 5052)

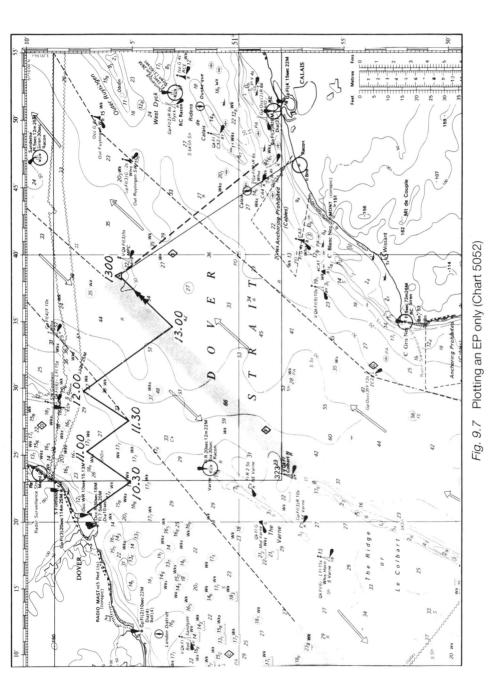

Fig. 9.7 Plotting an EP only (Chart 5052)

from the end of the DR plot. Remember that so long as the water track and tidal vectors are head to tail, we shall still get the same result.

Where do we go from here?

Once this is on, we have an EP for 13.00 hours and can check the situation. The best course we have been able to steer is 140 degrees. Allowing for leeway in an East wind, this gives us a practical course of 145 degrees over the water. What about tide now?

We have less than ten miles to go so it should take us under two hours. Between 13.00 and 14.00 the tide is still setting 040 degrees. From then on it will be setting 220 degrees but very weakly at first. The net result is still in a North East direction. Laying a course of 145 degrees from the EP will just pass the buoy. The tide will take us East of it. That is good, because we shall be up tide and up wind and will easily be able to adjust when we can see the buoy. The dotted lines in Figure 9.7 complete the passage.

Reflections

The last few paragraphs should have given you an idea of the kind of thinking required in chartwork. I have deliberately left a few questions unanswered. For example, both Figures 9.6 and 9.7 show the same journey under the same conditions (except the visibility). Tides, speeds and distances are *all* the same, they even finish in the same place at the same time. Why isn't the EP at 13.00 in the same place as the plot? Why is the fix at 11.05 so far from the plotted position? You should be able to answer these questions now. You should also be starting to understand how it is that you can sail to a place you can't see and actually get there.

Ship's log

The SHIP'S LOG and the RADIO LOG are the only records required by law. The former is a record of all things pertaining to the sailing of the vessel; course changes, wind strengths, sea state, barometer readings, visibility, sail changes, things sighted etc. etc. In the event of an enquiry into the conduct of the vessel, the log must be produced. Failure to do so will cause problems! It should be made up in pencil, which does not wash off if it gets soaked by a wave. Don't rub out though. Make any alterations by crossing out so that the original entry can still be read.

No hard and fast rules are laid down as to how often the log should be made up but most people do it hourly or two hourly. Since you will be rubbing your lines off the chart when they are finished with, it is the only permanent record that you will keep of what you did.

In the passage just made, we would have made entries each time the course was changed, as well as when we obtained a fix or worked out an EP.

The radio log is a similar document which records all radio messages sent and received by the vessel. It can also be demanded in the case of an enquiry.

These records should be maintained every time you are on passage, strictly every time you go to sea. Often your sailing will not be so much passage making as local sailing, or short hops port to port. These sorts of trips involve more pilotage than navigation, and this is the subject of the next chapter.

10

Pilotage

———————— ⚓ ————————

What you will learn

The marks available at sea for visual position finding.
   The IALA Buoyage system.
   The meanings and use of leading and clearing lines.
   The use of an echo sounder to find water depth and how soundings can help you.

When you have completed the chapter you will know

How to interpret chart information on lights.
   How to use navigational buoys.
   How to use leading and clearing lines to find a safe course.
   How a line of soundings can be used to find your position.

What you will need

A soft (2B) pencil and a ruler or straight edge.
   A pair of dividers and a protractor (or suitable substitutes).
   Preferably but not essentially, the Nautical Almanac you used in Chapters 6 and 7.

Pilotage is a form of navigation, but it is not concerned with plotting as in Chapter 9. It is a way of finding your way about using visual marks only. These marks may be natural or man-made.

In early sailing days, the only marks available were the natural ones provided by hills, river entrances, rocks etc. Gradually man-made objects such as houses, churches, breakwaters and so on, have become available. But all these were accidental; their primary job had nothing to do with finding one's way about at sea.

Lights

Beacons and lighthouses

The first significant change in thinking came quite early with the introduction of beacons and lighthouses. These, of course, were intended specifically for navigation. We do not know when the first beacon was lit, but we do know that the ancient Greeks had lighthouses. Curiously, day marks, which are a bit like lighthouses without lights, seem to have come later.

Chart information

Although only a full light list will give all the information there is to know about lights, most of what a yachtsman needs is right there on the chart. Not usually on a passage planning chart, but on any small or medium scale chart.

The information is always given in the same form and in the same order.

1st – The CHARACTERISTIC – The pattern of the flashes it sends out.

2nd – The COLOUR – The colour or colours, if it has more than one.

3rd – The PERIOD – The time taken to complete the sequence of the characteristic from the start of one cycle to the start of the next.

4th – The ELEVATION – The height of the actual light above mean high water springs.

5th – The RANGE – The distance over which the light can be seen in normal visibility.

The 4th and 5th items are only given for lighthouses and other lights where the elevation and range are significant. The elevation of a light can be used to find the distance from it when it just comes over the horizon. This is called the DIPPING DISTANCE and tables are provided in the almanacs for finding this. This can be very useful when you can just see the LOOM of a light. This is the bright halo that appears on the horizon shortly before the actual light is seen. It is clear enough to be able to identify the light and gets smaller as the light gets closer to the horizon, only to disappear just as the light comes into view.

A lower case 'm' is used for the elevation in metres and an upper case

'M' for the range in nautical miles. South Goodwin Lightship in Figure 9.2 shows an example of light data.

It is the 1st and 3rd items which make it possible to identify a particular light from all the others. The colours may be SECTORED, that is, visible over part of a circle only. This is particularly true of leading lights and to mark a danger area in relation to a lighthouse.

Buoyage

Buoys do not seem to have been invented so much as to have evolved. They probably started as floating barrels used by fishermen to indicate the deeper water in river estuaries. There is evidence to suggest that the shape of buoys derives from the practice of floating them on end on one side of a channel, and on their sides on the other.

The idea is to make buoys recognisable by day because of their shape and colour and by night because of the light pattern or characteristic that they flash. The possible colours and light patterns for particular buoys are laid down in a set of rules, the IALA system.

IALA system

Until quite recently there was no co-ordinated system of buoyage throughout the world. It was only in 1976, in Europe, that the system produced by the International Association of Light Authorities, was introduced. This is known as the IALA system. The IALA 'A' system is the one used in most of the world, with the 'B' system being confined, for the most part, to the Americas and Japan. The system is essentially simple and provides an internationally agreed method of marking waterways.

Cardinal buoys

The IALA system uses two main groups of buoys with a very few additional ones. The cardinal buoys are those which are used to mark the position of hazards in relation to the cardinal points of the compass; hence the name. Four buoys only are used, one in each of the four quadrants as shown in Figure 10.1.

In most cases, an individual danger can be marked by a single buoy, but occasionally two or more may be necessary. It is important to realise that the danger may lie anywhere within the quadrant and that the buoy is positioned on the side of the danger after which it is named. Thus a *North* cardinal buoy will be to the *North* of the danger, a *West* to the West and so on.

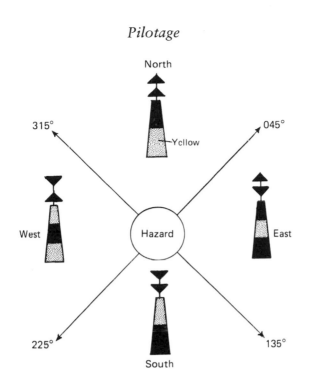

Fig. 10.1 Cardinal buoyage

Quadrant angles

The angles separating the quadrants are important because the danger may be extensive and *can* be found anywhere within the quadrant. This means that when passing a Cardinal Mark, you should pass it on the same side as its name. Pass North of a North cardinal mark, South of a South cardinal mark and so on. When going away from it, you will be clear of the danger so long as the bearing from the mark is outside the limits of its quadrant. Figure 10.2 should make this clear.

Lights

If you think of the cardinal system as a clock face, the light characteristics are easy to remember. The East is three o'clock and flashes three, the West is at nine o'clock and flashes nine. The South, at six o'clock flashes six but with an extra, long one, to make sure it is distinct from East and West. The North cardinal mark, at 12 o'clock, flashes continuously. These lights are all coloured white.

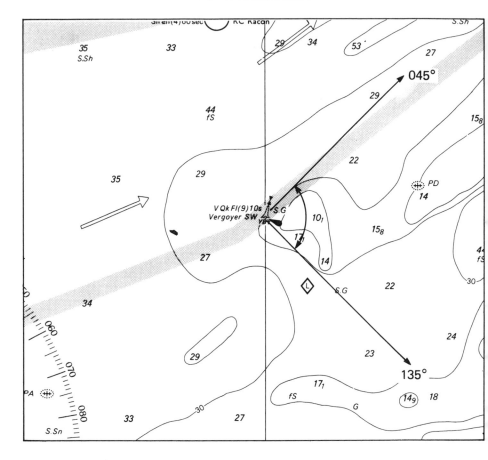

Fig. 10.2   Limits of hazard area of a West Cardinal buoy (Chart 5052)

Lateral marks

Buoys used to mark the limits of a channel are called lateral marks. Those placed on the port side going with the flood tide are coloured red, and those on the starboard side, green. Port hand marks have flat tops and are referred to as 'can shaped'. Starboard hand marks have pointed tops and are referred to as 'cone shaped'. Any lights are the same colour as the marks. The characteristics are usually groups of flashes from one to six, with odd numbers used on starboard and even numbers on port. These, and the next three types of mark, are illustrated in Figure 10.3.

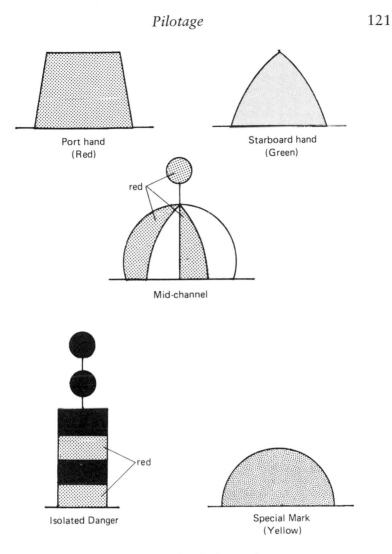

Fig. 10.3 Lateral and other marks

Mid-channel marks

Sometimes a spherical shaped buoy is used to mark the centre of a channel. This will be coloured red and white with the divisions marked vertically. It may have a red spherical top mark. Any light will be such that it is either ISOPHASE, which means having equal periods of light and dark, or OCCULTING which means that it is on most of the time with brief periods of darkness – 'flashes of darkness' as one of my students put it. Sometimes one long flash every ten seconds is used. These marks are sometimes called safe water marks.

Isolated danger marks

The exact opposite of safe water is the isolated danger mark. The thing to remember is that it has two black spheres as a top mark. Remember the two black ball shapes indicating aground in the rules? The mark is coloured red and black with horizontal bands. If it has two lights, the characteristic will be in groups of two flashes of white. An isolated danger is usually small in extent, such as a patch of rocks or a wreck.

Leading and Clearing Lines

In Chapter 9 I talked about transits as special position lines. In pilotage, transits are particularly useful. Where they are used as LEADING LINES, specifically intended to guide you into or out of a restricted channel, they are sometimes actually drawn on Admiralty charts; if they are not you can always draw your own. Linking a buoy with a church or other conspicuous building can often save you a good deal of time with the compass. In some instances such a line can be used as a leading line to guide you in or out. At other times it may be used as a CLEARING LINE, in the manner: 'As long as I stay to port of that line, I shall miss the rocks.'

Leading and clearing lines can often be particularly useful when there is a strong cross tide, as a way of checking that you are actually sailing the line you think you are. Pilot books often include them. The chartlet showing the entry to Salcombe in Devon in Figure 10.4 is taken from the *Cruising Association Handbook* and shows leading and clearing lines, as well as beacons.

BEACONS, which take the form of painted posts, small pillars, towers or even painted patches on rocks are useful aids to pilotage, but you need to know what they mean! This information can sometimes be found on the chart but more often you will need to use SAILING DIRECTIONS. They are sometimes used to mark dangers but more often are the marks for leading lines as in Figure 10.4.

Sailing directions

These are, as their name suggests, directions on how to sail in a particular location. They are to be found in many places. Figure 7.2 showed the useful, if brief, sailing directions that appear in an almanac. Admiralty publications, such as the various *pilots*, provide excellent sailing directions. These tend to be directed towards big ships and may not be as useful to yachtsmen as the special 'yachtsmen's pilots' of which there are so many.

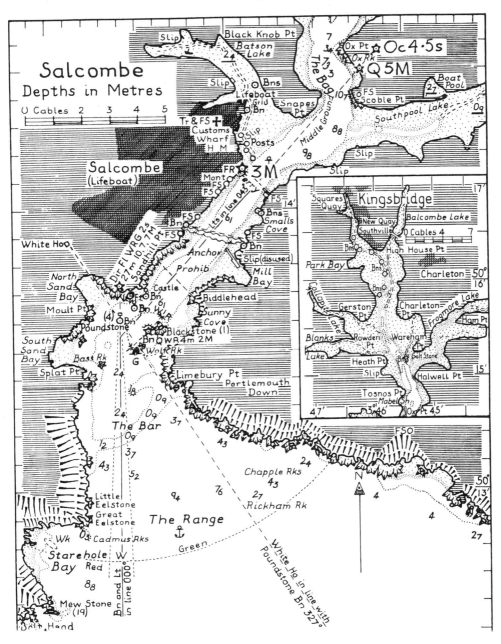

Fig. 10.4 Leading and clearing lines

This subject was mentioned in Chapter 6 but is worth bringing up again since they are so useful. You will find all kinds of information about useful transits, leading and clearance lines and so on in them. Minor channels, marked only by sticks put in by locals, may even be described in these books.

Sailing directions will also tell you about unusual tide sets, the shift of sand bars, moorings, where the ferries run and all manner of useful information. Don't wait until you are on your way into a strange harbour before looking at them. If you plan to visit a new place, you can be sure someone has been there before, and written about it.

Overfalls

OVERFALLS are a feature that is sometimes shown on the chart and often mentioned in sailing directions. They are caused by the tide passing over a shallower area of the sea bed such as may be found extending out from a headland. The effect is to cause steep and choppy seas which are best avoided, particularly when the wind and tide are working in opposite directions. This is referred to as a wind-over-tide situation and if the wind is at all strong, can produce dangerous conditions. On charts, their presence is indicated by groups of short wavy lines.

Pilotage Planning

Quite apart from learning as much as you can about a strange harbour or anchorage before you visit it, the more you can plan your pilotage in the comfort of your armchair, the better prepared you will be. When the time starts to go in on a wild and windy night, this forethought will repay you handsomely.

Selection of essentials

If the place you are going to is a busy port, it will have many buoys, leading lights, beacons etc. They will generally be intended for large vessels with a draught much more than yours and a lot of them will be of little interest to you. Try to decide in advance which ones *will matter to you*. You can then list these in the order in which you expect to see them. You can also check that your chart (you will need a small-scale harbour chart) has been corrected up to date. It can be very unnerving to find, when you are half-way up a channel, that the buoy you were depending on to tell you when to turn, has been removed or altered. This really gets the adrenalin going!

I always mark on my list the compass bearing from the buoy I am about to tick off, to the next one. It saves that horrible moment when you can't see the next mark and the helmsman, with a note of panic in his voice, says: 'What do I do now?' If you can immediately answer: 'Steer 045 and look for a green light', it gives the impression that you know what you are doing even if *you* don't! It also helps tremendously if visibility is a bit down.

Part of pilotage is not hitting the bottom, as well as not hitting the sides. All that stuff from Chapter 7 about finding how much water you have under the keel *now* begins to pay off. You should have done all the anticipating on this score long before you arrived at your destination, or even before you left home. After all, you know on what *day* you will arrive at your destination, so you can do the job for the 12-hour period during which you expect to get there.

Echo sounding

Keeping a check on the depth when in confined waters makes sense. Running aground is something that we all do sooner or later, but if you are careful you can postpone the day. Sometimes, when the channel you are following is well charted but not well marked, the taking of depth readings may be the only way to pilot yourself along it.

Using soundings

With modern types of sounding equipment you may have a shallow water alarm and so do not actually have to watch the instrument all the time. You simply look at the chart and check the least depth at which you will be safe, allow a margin for safety and set the alarm. When you get into water that is below this depth, the alarm sounds. The snag with this method is that you do not always know in which direction to turn in order to get back into deeper water. If you can arrange it, it is better to have someone watching the SOUNDINGS who can call out 'shallowing' or 'deepening' as the case may be. This information is often of more use than the actual depth.

Don't use the words 'rising' and 'falling'. They are open to misinterpretation. You may see rising as the boat getting higher above the sea bed, whereas your checker may see it as the bottom coming up to meet the boat. This sort of ambiguity you can well do without. In a really tricky situation once, off the coast of Brittany in thick fog, I found that the actual words did not matter at all. I was able to pilot on the pitch of the caller's voice, which rose and fell with the depth of the water!

Line of soundings

A line of soundings is mentioned in many books under 'position fixing'. It is more a pilotage technique than navigation, I feel.

In poor visibility, when you cannot see the shore, it is possible, provided that you know approximately where you are, to approach the shore safely using the echo-sounder and to find your way in. To do so requires that the sea bed is uneven rather than flat and that there is a clear change in depth at the point you wish to approach and enter.

The method is to steer a steady course at a steady *slow* speed and to take depth readings at regular intervals, say every quarter or half mile. If you have prepared a strip of paper with its edge marked to scale at the same intervals as you are using, you can write each depth against each successive mark. Calculate the tide height and allow for this. Now take the strip of paper and lay it on the chart in the direction of your course line. You should be able, if the bottom is uneven, to find some point where your strip fits the charted depths. This will give your position when the last reading was taken. It is not a very accurate method but I have used it with success to pilot myself in, when nothing else was available. If even one other position line can be produced, the accuracy goes up a good deal.

Aiming off

If you are in fog and have to round a headland with shallow water surrounding it, before turning in it is a good idea to aim off; that is to aim off course deliberately, aiming *for* the headland rather than to clear it. By doing this, you will know in which direction to turn when you reach the shallow water and can then follow a safe contour all round. In this way, you will avoid missing the headland altogether and being obliged to turn in, now knowing which side of it you are.

The same technique can be used when approaching shore after a long passage. If you aim off, up tide, you will know which side of your objective you are when you reach the coast, and can then turn down tide and follow the coast until you find your destination.

Bad visibility

In fog or even heavy rain, piloting can become an exciting pastime. If you are close to the shore when caught in such conditions you should consider stopping. The best way to avoid being hit by a ship is to be in water too shallow for it. If you are piloting in misty conditions, and are in a busy area or are uncertain where you are, the wise thing to do is to head for shallow water and put down your anchor. You can then sit it out until the visibility improves. A live coward is better than a dead hero.

Anchorages

This brings me to another point. Many people who are used to sailing from marina to marina, neglect the anchor and thereby miss a great deal. In some places, thank God, it is still possible to find a place to stop that is not full of boats tied up to lumps of iron and concrete.

Many small-scale charts, and almost all pilot books, will tell you of places where you can put down your own hook and stay, free from worldly cares, although you may be charged for the privilege. When you have gained in experience you will be able to find some of the more rewarding spots that are not charted for yourself.

What should you look for? The first thing is good holding ground. If the bottom is firm sand or mud you will stand a pretty good chance of holding, especially if you choose a place which is sheltered with an offshore wind. If you intend to stay overnight you will need to check the forecasts. Make sure that you will not ground at low tide. This means checking not just where you anchor, but also a small circle round so that as you turn with the tide you do not fetch up on some rock of which you were unaware.

The best thing is to approach at low tide if you can. In this way you will be able to see likely dangers and, if you do touch, you will soon float off. Looking for an anchorage in a place you do not know, on a falling tide, is asking for trouble.

Do not forget your anchor ball signal when you have stopped. It is often very difficult for someone on a fast moving vessel to tell if a yacht is stopped or just motoring slowly. Also, take a couple of bearings or find a couple of natural transits so that you can check your position from time to time. This is part of the job.

A few pilotage tips

Pilotage tends to be a fraught activity. When you are nervously approaching a strange place and are looking for something to identify, it is very easy to fall into a trap. This is the trap of making what you *actually* see become what you *want* to see. Many enquiries into groundings, even with big ships, find that the trouble comes from the vessels not being where they thought they were.

If the facts do not fit – beware! Look for a reason, do not change the facts.

For the above reason, when you are looking for a particular mark or light, do not tell your crew what it actually is, get them to help look for it but give them a general description such as, 'a red flashing light somewhere on the bow'. When they say they can see it, ask them to tell you its characteristic and period. This will make sure you have the right one. Don't say 'on the port bow'. They may not look to starboard if you do and, if it *is* on the *wrong* side, this could matter a lot!

Have it all planned; the fewer surprises the better! Piloting should be pleasing and satisfying, not panicky and scaring.

11

Electronic Sailing

———————— ⚓ ————————

What you will learn

Some of the advances in electronic technology that have been developed in recent years as they apply to pleasure boating.

By the time you have completed this chapter you will have

A good idea of what is available to you and how it can be used as well as its limitations.

What you will need

No additional items will be needed to study this chapter, but you will get the most from it after you have studied Chapters 7 and 8.

A caution

Before discussing electronic aids to sailing, one thing must be said. It is my belief that the specialised aids, such as Decca etc, should not be used by anyone who can not navigate effectively without them. It is a dangerous practice to fit such a device and then to rely on it without making any provision for its failure.

A recent example illustrates the point. The weather was fine with a Force 3 wind and visibility about six or seven miles. A yacht was heard calling the Coastguard. When he got through the following conversation ensued.

'Windswept Coastguard. This is yacht Foolhardy. My Decca has gone on the blink. Can you tell me where we are?'

'Yacht Foolhardy. Windswept Coastguard. Give me a count of ten. Over.'

'One, two, three, . . . nine, ten. Over.'

'Yacht Foolhardy. Windswept Coastguard. Can you see the coast? Over.'

'Yacht Foolhardy. Yes. Over'

'Foolhardy. Windswept Coastguard. May I suggest you follow it until you can see something you recognise? Over.'

We heard no reply to the last transmission. The Coastguard had been as courteous as always.

The point about this exchange is that the yacht in question had clearly been relying entirely on his Decca and had been keeping no DR position going. Had he been keeping even a two hourly note of his Decca position together with a note of course steered and speed, either on the chart or in the ship's log, he would have known where he was well within the visibility range of six miles.

Such a failure is irresponsible, if not actually dangerous. His call was really an abuse of the Coastguard facility as well as being a very poor advertisement for all yachtsmen. In the face of myriads of idiot calls, I have never heard a Coastguard reply other than with politeness. The irony on this occasion must have delighted many other listeners in the area, as it did me.

One wonders what would have happened to that particular yacht if conditions had been bad and his VHF had failed along with his Decca. Electronics are only as good as the power supply after all. They are also only as good as the people operating them.

Log and depth sounder

These devices are electronic aids but have been discussed elsewhere in this book, and so will not be discussed again here, although they are part of the electronic aid system.

VHF radio

In the anecdote above, the yacht skipper was trying to use one of the facilities now available from the Coastguard. The Coastguard stations operate over a large area by means of multiple aerials spaced along the coast, so it is possible for them to give a DF bearing of a transmitting station from their aerial. The accuracy of such a bearing will not be high (a bearing stated as Class C is within plus or minus 10 degrees, for example) but it can serve as a useful indicator in emergency.

It should, of course, not be used primarily as a navigational aid. The emphasis must be on emergency. Imagine what would happen on a summer afternoon if everyone relied on Coastguard stations for fixing their position!

The main purpose of Marine VHF is for keeping in touch; for getting news of weather, advising of movements and safe arrival; for calling for help when you really need it, and for learning when other people need help. Now that it is in common use on yachts, it has saved many lives, but be brief and do not waste air time, or the system will become far less useful.

Position Fixing Devices

Radio Direction Finding (RDF)

The RDF instrument is actually a simple radio receiver with a directional aerial and a compass to tell you where the aerial is pointing. Signals are transmitted in the long wave band from beacons in various locations. One frequency is allocated to up to six beacons, each of which transmits its signal in turn at precise times. The signal consists of a Morse Code identity followed by a continuous tone and then a repetition of the identity signal. Each total transmission lasts one minute and is repeated at six minute intervals.

Receivers vary in complexity (and cost). The more complex versions have synthesised tuners which make finding a particular chain easier and usually a visual as well as audible means of finding the NULL or minimum signal. The compass is arranged to give a bearing when the minimum signal is received since this is easier for the human ear to detect than the maximum. Some instruments have an integral clock which enables them to tell you which beacon in the chain you are using.

Using RDF

The instrument is used in the same way as a hand bearing compass with the advantage that it 'sees' a great deal further and in poor visibility. Accuracy however is deceptive since a number of errors are inherent. The worst of these occur at twilight and when the signal passes over land. Atmospheric conditions can also affect the signal. As a back up for visual observations and as an aid in poor visibility RDF has its uses but it is rapidly being superseded by the more sophisticated systems of position fixing described below.

Decca navigators

The Decca system (the name refers both to the makers and the principle) was originally developed during the Second World War from an American idea of 1937. It was intended for naval use and played an important part in war-time secret operations. It is based on interpretation of the relationships between a number of radio signals transmitted by fixed shore stations. In its original form, special charts were needed and skill was required to use it. These facts, coupled to the large size of the equipment and its high rental cost, prevented yachts from taking advantage of the facility.

With the advent of computer technology, the whole thing changed. The difficult bit could be done by a small onboard computer and the answer wanted, one's position, could be displayed directly on a LCD screen. Size was reduced to that of a modest book, power consumption became low and use of the instrument was very simple. Cost also came down. A once-only payment to include a licence component was charged, and yachts quickly started to fit the aid.

All seemed perfect. Not so! Other manufacturers started producing the device, or rather similar devices which used the Decca chains of shore stations. Decca, who ran and maintained the shore stations, were understandably peeved and legal wrangles began. The end result has been that Government has now agreed to take over the running of the shore-based part of the system into the next decade, and other producers are being allowed to compete with Decca for the on-board instruments. The location of shore stations means that the system is available over most of Europe.

Loran

Loran is a similar system to Decca, developed in America at about the same time. It works on a different, though similar principle, which makes it rather more accurate at greater ranges than Decca, but at present very few shore stations exist in Northern Europe, so that it is of practical use only in the Mediterranean and Scandinavia as well as North America. It seems likely that more European stations will be installed and we may have Loran available in UK waters shortly.

Satellite systems

Such systems are based on the use of satellites in orbit round the earth. The limitation of the Transit system in use at the moment, relates to the number of satellites available. Whilst the data is very accurate, fixes are possible only at relatively long intervals, about 90 mins apart in the UK. The effect is that although the system is more accurate and less subject to degradation than either Decca or Loran, it is only of practical use on ocean passages at the moment.

The Transit system was intended to be replaced by a new system called GPS (Global Positioning System) towards the end of the 1980s. The whole satellite programme was badly affected by the Shuttle disaster which has caused a great delay in getting satellites into orbit. When the GPS system does come into operation it will be extremely accurate to the extent that it is intended that the civilian version will be downgraded. Position fixing should be possible to within 100m at any time and anywhere in the world.

The future

Decca will survive at least until the mid-1990s with government backing, whilst Loran will probably become more widely available in Europe. When the GPS system is fully operational it is likely to become the primary system in relation to the existing systems but not replace them entirely. This will probably be by the late 1990s. There is a suggestion that either Decca, Loran or both will still be around until the end of the century.

Relative merits

Decca gives good coverage in UK waters but is subject to the same degradations as any other radio transmissions in the mid-frequency band, because of the way such signals travel. This reduces the quality of signal, and thus accuracy, particularly around dawn and dusk. Decca also suffers from atmospheric and other interference. All these together effectively limit its range to about 240 miles from the transmitter. It does generally get more accurate as you get closer to land, which is useful.

Loran, as mentioned earlier, is limited in Europe by the lack of ground stations but is an inherently more accurate system, particularly at longer ranges, and is less subject to interference. It does generate some of its own interference, however, which has limited its popularity.

The satellite systems should be regarded, by home waters sailors, as a thing of the future rather than a present aid.

What they do

The primary function of all the position-indicating devices, is to provide an updated position in terms of latitude and longitude. This has resulted in a change in the way of recording a vessel's position. Latitude and longitude were previously little used by small vessel navigators. Because the information is updated several times a minute, at least in Decca and Loran, they can also be made to do many other things. The limit really depends on the inventiveness of the particular instrument's designer.

I have tried two types, Decca 3 and Navstar 2000D, both of which use the Decca chains. I will therefore use these to indicate the possibilities. Loran provides similar outputs to the Decca based systems.

The clock

The incorporation of an accurate clock enables the devices to derive speeds from a series of position changes. This means it can tell you how fast you are going and make estimates of how long it will take to reach your destination or some intermediate point on the way. It also provides an alarm clock, which is useful.

Waypoints

A waypoint is a specific location on a passage at which you wish to do something; arrive, change direction and so on. A route will thus consist of a succession of waypoints. It is possible with both instruments, to enter a number of waypoints in advance. A group of these (up to 25) can then be put together in any desired order to form a route.

You can store several routes in memory with Navstar and select the one you want or you can make up a new route using the bank of stored waypoints. With Decca 3 you only hold one route in memory at a time.

Navigating with waypoints

When navigating a particular route using either instrument, it will give you a course to steer and a distance from your present position to the next waypoint. You can also find your actual course over the ground, your speed, and any deviation from the rhumb line course. Variation can be included and, with Navstar Deviation also, so that the course to steer can be compass if you wish. Navstar also allows you to include a tidal vector.

From this you can see that the temptation to rely only on the instruments can be great!

Errors and alarms

Both instruments are self checking and will let you know, by means of alarms, if the signal quality is not good enough to provide accurate positions. They also have alarms to let you know when you are close to your next waypoint and when you have moved on to the next leg of your route. To make the best use of this error information requires a knowledge of how the signals are produced.

Chains

Each position is derived from information transmitted by a group of shore stations called a chain. A master station and normally three so-called slave stations can normally be received. The instruments are programmed to select the appropriate chain and the best pair of slave signals automatically as the vessel moves from one area to another. This automatic facility may be overridden if desired and this can be useful. To work, the instrument has to be given an initial position, which must be correct to within about two miles, so that it can select the correct chain.

Beware the dangers

The obvious one is that you must record progress so that in the event of total failure you can revert to manual navigation. In practice this means, as a minimum, putting rhumb lines on your chart and recording your position at regular intervals, together with course steered and speed. You will then be able to carry on with DR from your last known position if you have to.

The Decca System can occasionally produce a false position. This can happen if your instrument is calculating your position using the wrong data, either because it did not know where you were when you started or because it has jumped lanes on route. You can reduce the risk of the first happening, and you can make it easier to spot the second if it does happen.

First, make sure that you enter an accurate position (correct to within two miles) when you start your passage. Then leave the instrument on whenever you are moving so that it keeps track of any changes. Second, look at your last position each time you record a new one, especially when moving from one chain area to another. Any error will be gross (at least 10 km) and will thus be easily spotted since the position change will be inconsistent with your movements.

Radar

Let it be said at the outset that radar is not primarily a position fixing system. It stands for Radio Assisted Direction And Ranging. It tells you in what direction and how far something is from you. From this you can deduce your position. Again it was a war-time invention and, until the advent of micro-electronics, out of the reach of most yachtsmen.

Early systems had to be viewed in near darkness or with the use of a hood and were costly and had high power consumption. All this has now changed and many examples for yacht use can be found. Most are for daylight viewing and several now have such things as raster scanning, electronic simulated imaging, image enhancement etc.

I do not intend to explain these terms here. The subject of radar really needs a book of its own. Those readers who are interested will find many to choose from.

The principles

Radar works by transmitting an extremely short-wave radio signal in very brief pulses. The signal is reflected to varying degrees off different materials. Some of this reflected signal is detected when it gets back to the instrument. By measuring both the time taken for the signal to return and the direction from which it comes, then displaying this information on a suitable screen, a picture can be drawn in light, showing the positions of the things that reflected the signal.

Only very small amounts of signal are returned so these have to be greatly amplified. This, together with the fact that not all materials reflect signals, results in a rather crude picture. Such pictures need some practice to interpret correctly.

The signal is transmitted in the form of a narrow beam the width of which affects the resolution of the image. For example, a small cove or river entrance may not be seen on the screen at all if the beam covers both sides of the gap. Very narrow beam radar is still not feasible for small vessel use.

Unfortunately rain and sea spray reflect the signals quite well and can obscure a more solid target behind them! Modern instruments have some very nifty circuitry to get round this problem and it is becoming a less serious one, although removing unwanted signals always has some adverse effect on the wanted ones.

Using radar

The foregoing is not intended to suggest that radar is no use. It is just to show that to use it is not by any means as easy as using the other things mentioned.

The greatest benefits for most radar users are considered to be the ability to locate buoys or to make a landfall in poor visibility and, above all, the ability to see things not on the chart. The most important of these is other vessels – especially those that are moving.

Relative motion

The big difficulty when using radar in collision avoidance is not always obvious to the user. For practical reasons as well as those of cost, small boat radar is almost always 'relative motion radar' with 'head up display'. When you look at the display on the screen of such a radar you are looking at a birds' eye view. Your position on the display is fixed, usually at the centre but occasionally at the bottom of the screen and the direction of travel (ship's heading) is directly towards the top of the screen. It is the exact opposite of looking at your progress on a chart in that, with radar, you appear static whilst everything else moves. The thing is that, because you are really moving, your actual position in absolute terms is constantly changing. This has important repercussions in interpreting the display.

I will use an example to show the problem. Suppose you look at the display and notice a target object on the display, perhaps a ship, five miles distant on a bearing of 045 degrees to starboard. Ten minutes later you look again and see that the target is now only four miles distant with the same bearing. What is happening? Instinct tells you that you are closing the other vessel on a constant bearing. A collision situation? Not necessarily. The bearing you are measuring on the radar is a bearing relative to the ship's heading at the time and not a true bearing. It is similar to making an estimate on a visual sighting rather than using a hand bearing compass. If you have made a slight course change between taking the two readings then this will have the effect of rotating all the images on the screen.

Imagine the screen as a window looking down on a chart over which you are moving. You, the observer, are looking through the centre of the window. The top of the window always points in the direction in which the vessel is moving so that as you progress in a straight line, the chart appears to roll downwards under your eye. If your vessel turns, the chart appears to rotate. Thus for an object to maintain a constant bearing from the centre of the window, it must have a component of its motion equal and opposite to the motion of the chart (remember the chess board in Chapter 7?).

For the bearing and range to remain constant the target must thus be moving in the same direction *and* at the same speed as the observer. Any change in range represents a component in the movement of the target resulting from a difference in relative velocities (a velocity has both speed and direction). Remember that a stationary object such as a buoy or anchored vessel will appear to move down the screen so its bearing will change. The observer's motion is always a component vector. To find a target's true motion, both the component vectors must be drawn and the resultant measured.

Consider that the last paragraph assumes the courses and speeds of both observer and target to have remained constant. In practice, one should always take three observations before making such assumptions. As each observation is made a careful note of one's own heading and speed must be recorded since even quite small changes can distort the results.

The problem should now be apparent. Plotting by radar involves both time and careful calculation. Often, in possible collision situations, time is not available. It also means that in bad visibility one person is needed to be plotting constantly. If you have radar, Rule 7 of the International Regulations *requires* you to use it in poor visibility. You can not opt out.

Radar or not?

Many small boats have fitted radar and more will do so. Cost is coming down and quality improving. I have tried to show that there is more to the subject than meets the eye. If you sail on a boat fitted with radar you must be sure that you know how to use it so that you do not contribute to one of the so called 'radar assisted collisions'.

I am not saying do not have radar. I am saying that if you do have it, you must know how to use it and be in a position to do so when required.

Conclusions

The electronic aids available to sailors are increasing rapidly in number whilst becoming both cheaper and more sophisticated. The best advice I can give you is still the same. Make sure that you have a good understanding of the basics of navigation so that you can work out where you are. Be sure you understand the rules and principles for avoiding collisions so that you can sail safely. If you have the electronics available, treat them as aids and not as substitutes for good seamanship. Make sure that you know how to use them properly so that they will be true aids rather than hindrances.

12

Planning a Passage

_____ ⚓ _____

What you will learn

The things that need to be considered when planning a passage.

By the time you have completed this chapter you will know

How to obtain an up to date weather forecast.
 What tidal information you will need for planning.
 How to decide what charts and publications you are going to need.
 What stores to think about.
 The safety precautions to take before departure.

What you will need

No special equipment is needed for this chapter.

Planning a passage is an exciting exercise in itself. It is all too easy, when doing it, to get so carried away that you do far too much planning!

Of *course* planning is important and, in a sense, you *can't* do too much. What often happens is a failure to plan the planning. This results in doing some things that would be better not done at the expense of things that are vital. So, what should go into the planning?

There are three questions that you need to ask yourself under this heading:

1 Can I get the boat out from where it is now, when I want to?
2 Can I get it into where I am going, at the time when I expect to arrive?
3 How long will it take to cover the middle bit, and what happens there?

Weather

This is a crucial subject. It will usually decide whether you go at all. I could have devoted a whole chapter, or even a whole book, to it. In this book I will not try to turn you into a weather expert, I will simply tell you how to get the information you need.

As soon as any passage is contemplated, you need to start making an appreciation of the weather situation. It is no good coming down to the boat in the morning and saying: 'It's a lovely day. Let's go to Gogmagog.' Especially if Gogmagog is a day or more's sailing away.

Fortunately, with modern weather information, it is possible to get a very good idea of what is likely to happen for several days ahead. If the forecaster says: 'Things are looking unsettled. I cannot give you much idea of what to expect over the next few days', that is your information! It means, it would be best to postpone the trip for a while. Unless you intend to go ocean voyaging, this is all you need.

Forecasts

Still sitting at home, there are several ways to find out what the weather is going to be. Broadcast forecasts are put out by radio and television at regular times. The times are given in newspapers, in published timetables and in almanacs, together with the frequencies and channels.

Shipping forecasts

Shipping forecasts are broadcast four times a day on Radio 4 1500 metres, long wave. This broadcast can be heard over all the northern European sea areas that it covers, from Iceland to northern Spain. Similar broadcasts are made by most national networks round the world. They need to be understood to be useful. The terms used are very precise but not always immediately obvious.

Beaufort scale

Wind speeds in forecasts are given in terms of the Beaufort scale. In Force 1 you will not have enough wind to sail most boats whilst Force 6 is generally considered the 'yachtsman's gale' although, with superb understatement, Admiral Beaufort described it as a 'Strong Breeze'. Winds of Force 3 or 4 will get you going well and, in summer, are probably the most enjoyable.

Without practice, it is very difficult to write down all the forecast information. It is a good idea both to practise at home, and to carry a portable tape recorder on board so that you can record and play back if you need to. The two forecasts put out at 00.33 and at 05.50 are at rather anti-social times and only the former gives the full inshore forecast. It is this inshore forecast, which covers coastal waters, that is the most useful.

Local radio

Local radio weather information is often of more use to the coastal sailor than the shipping forecasts. It is broadcast at less anti-social hours for a start. It often gives the local sea areas, the inshore (within about six miles of the coast) forecast, as well as actual sea conditions in the area.

Television

The thing I like about the television weather broadcasts are the maps. Once you have learned to understand these, you can get a very good idea of what to expect for several days ahead. The explanation given is for the layman and is clear. Particularly useful are the probable wind speeds and directions; these are so important to sailors.

Telephone

The 'Weatherline' system which has been in operation for the past few years, is a useful service for yachtsmen. Run jointly by British Telecom, the Coastguard Service and *Practical Boat Owner* magazine, it gives the latest inshore forecast for a large number of coastal areas for the price of a 'phone call at any time. You can 'phone your destination area as well as your local one for news. If you have a local meteorological station, they will usually be pleased to help over the 'phone, although some get very busy in the summer.

VHF channel 67

If you have VHF on your boat, you will find that the Coastguard gives out weather news on channel 67 after first announcing the intention on channel 16. If you have VHF, you should be listening on channel 16 all the time for emergency calls! Coast radio stations also provide weather information at set times each day.

General

The idea is to use as many sources of weather information as you can as a part of your passage planning, and also to update this information whilst actually on passage. If you do, you are unlikely to be caught out very often.

It is a good idea to learn to anticipate local changes which may affect you; the build up of cloud and how to recognise fronts for example. *Instant Weather Forecasting* by Allan Watts, published by Adlard Coles, is a useful book for beginners in this subject.

I have deliberately concentrated on where to get forecasts with only the merest hints on interpretation. This is because you must *experience* weather at sea in relation to the forecasts before you can *fully* understand them. This need not happen too soon if you follow the advice I have given. Start by being a fair weather sailor, it makes sense.

Certainly when you start sailing, and probably for a long time afterwards, the weather is going to be the main consideration as to whether you go or not. It will also be the least predictable.

Tides

All three of the questions at the beginning of this chapter are concerned with tides. Your planning notebook should include enough so that you don't need to search through the almanac whilst on passage. This means that you will need the following:

1 Times and heights of high water at the reference port for the tidal atlas or diamonds that you are using. Beware of using the wrong one. Just as an example Dover and Devonport have high waters 5 hours and 40 minutes apart. Both are used as reference ports on English Channel charts. The wrong choice would mean that the stream sets are almost reversed!

2 Times and heights of both high and low waters at the standard port for your departure port. Also at the standard port for your destination as well as any other ports you intend to visit.

3 The differences that apply, to both times and heights, at all the secondary ports you are going to and also those which you may use in an emergency (see Fig. 12.1).

4 How the dates on which you are sailing relate to spring and neap tides on either side.

Armed with all this data, you are ready to start. Figure 12.1 shows a form of layout suitable for calculating the heights and times at secondary ports. The instructions for using it are in Figure 12.2. The calculations should be done for all the ports you will visit during the passage. It is not necessary to do them too far ahead. The idea is not to have to do them at sea, so if you are going to be in port for a while, you can do the next ones after you arrive.

TIDAL PREDICTION FORM					
Date: Local time is: GMT / BST / GMT +/- hr(s)					A
H.W. at Tidal Atlas Port Date/Time: Date/Time: (Name):					B
Standard Port 1:					C
	Time (GMT)	Height (m)	Time (GMT)	Height (m)	
High Water					D
Low Water					E
Range					F
Standard Port 2:					G
	Time	Height	Time	Height	
High Water					H
Low Water					I
Range					J
Secondary Port 1: Differences on:					K
	Time	Height	Time	Height	
High Water					L
Low Water					M
Range					N
Entry/Exit possible from: to:					O
Secondary Port 2: Differences on:					P
	Time	Height	Time	Height	
High Water					Q
Low Water					R
Range					S
Entry/Exit possible from: to:					T
Alternate Port 1: Differences on:					U
	Time	Height	Time	Height	
High Water					V
Low Water					W
Range					X
Entry/Exit possible from: to:					Y
Alternate Port 2: Differences on:					Z
	Time	Height	Time	Height	
High Water					a
Low Water					b
Range					c
Entry/Exit possible from: to:					d

Fig. 12.1 Tidal Prediction form

Do not forget to use the graph, as we did in Chapter 7, to find the earliest and latest times you can go in to *all* possible destinations on *this* passage. It *is* worthwhile to do the calculations for any emergency ports. The last thing you want to be doing, if you have been forced to change your plans by bad weather, is to be sitting below trying to work out if you have enough water to get in!

Instructions for completing Tidal Prediction Form

1   Enter the date of the projected passage on line A also delete as appropriate so that local time is indicated. If the local time at any port to be visited is different from line A, note the difference in the appropriate box, lines K, P, U, Z.
2   Now enter the port named in the tidal atlas you are using at B and enter the dates and times required.
3   Both C and G are available for Standard port information.
4   Next complete the boxes on lines D and E, also H and I if needed.
5   Subtract the heights in lines E and I from those in lines D and H to find the range.
6   Now look up the differences between the chosen standard ports and the secondary ports on lines K, P, U and Z.
7   In turn calculate the High and Low water times and Heights at each secondary port and enter them in the appropriate boxes.
8   After checking, apply these figures to the Standard Port curves to find the Entry and Exit limitations and enter these on lines O, T, Y and D. If there are no limits note this down.

Notes
1. This form contains a great deal of information in a very small space. It is only as useful as it is accurate so check each entry carefully.
2. If you anticipate arriving at a port on a *different date* to your starting date, record this fact in the name box on lines G, K, P, U or Z and enter data for the *relevant* date.

Fig. 12.2   Instructions for completing Tidal Prediction form

Charts and Publications

As discussed in Chapter 6, you must have charts. You can't plot positions or know precisely where you are without them. The question is, which ones? You cannot possibly have them all; you wouldn't get them in your boat.

The best solution to this is to start with the minimum and work up. You will need a passage planning chart. It makes life so much easier if you can see both ends of the journey on the same chart. You will also have to have charts covering each end which are of a small enough scale to have the important things marked on them. They will also be used for more accurate plotting as you are close to each end of the passage. Harbour charts will be needed for close work when you actually go in or out. The chartlets in the almanac are often quite good for this and save money. When you have your own boat, you will gradually build up a portfolio of charts covering the areas in which you sail. They must all be kept up to date.

I have mentioned emergency alternatives before. It is always a good idea to plan for problems rather than to wait until they happen. The emergency may be only a little one, or it may be serious, but whatever it is, it could make you change your plans.

Good planning means you will have an alternative destination, or possibly several, that you could use. If these are not on your 'end' charts you will need extra charts to cover these alternatives.

I also like to have charts that go a bit outside the area that I mean to be in. You *can* get pushed well off your intended course by bad weather. You do not want to be forced to beat into a gale when you could have run down wind, if only you had had the right chart.

Pilot books

Apart from charts and an almanac, tide tables and a tidal atlas, you will need to have with you, and to have studied, at least one pilot book. I keep a note in my planning of which books, together with page numbers, that I might use. Those that I *intend* to use I flag with paper strips with the name of the place written on the top. This saves time.

I also like to make sure that any changes in buoyage etc., that I have got from 'M' notices on my chart, are included in the pilot. Admiralty sailing directions do have corrections published from time to time, as do *some* yachting pilot books. It is unreasonable to expect a pilot to be bang up to date. The information it contains may have been collected over a period of a year or more. It then has to be written and published. If you respect its limitations, a pilot is of great value. But remember, checking is up to you.

Pilotage

Pilotage planning has been discussed in Chapter 10. It should include, as well as the getting-in-and-out-bits, a list of any lighthouses and radio beacons you may use, together with their identification characteristics. I like to note any conspicuous landmarks that might be of use and any dangers on the route such as shallows, shipping lanes and so on, that will call for extra vigilance. I then make a note of the probable log readings I anticipate, and of the times when I expect to get to them.

Victualling

Now there is a real old seafarers' word! It is usually applied to the inner man but, if you are responsible for victualling a boat it means a lot more. It means making sure that both the vessel and the crew have all that they need to fuel them until they get to their destination, whatever happens. This includes water and fuel as well as food.

Food

What food you take depends on a lot of things. How long the passage will be and what chances you will have for replenishing stocks. Personal preferences of the crew will matter also. When planning always add a margin for delays. One day's reserve is normally enough for coastal sailing.

Always plan for at least one main hot cooked meal each day. If it is to be prepared at sea, a one-pot meal is easiest. This can then be supplemented with frequent snacks and hot drinks, soup and so on. Do not look to produce elaborate meals that are rich or involve lots of pans. This will not work at sea. Appetites are often a little jaded and food needs to be tasty, but neither too strong nor too rich. There is at least one individual said to have circumnavigated the world on a diet exclusively of curry and porridge! I do not recommend it though.

Little and often seems to work best. A supply of easy foods such as biscuits, cake, fruit, nuts and chocolate are good if the weather gets unkind. Flasks of boiling water for drinks, rather than trying to boil kettles is a help in such conditions. The invention of soups that can be made in a cup has been a great boon to yachtsmen.

If you do cook at sea, always wear oilskin trousers to protect against scalds. Even on a mooring or in a marina you must remember you are on an inherently unstable platform.

Fuel and water

This subject includes fuel for both the main and any standby engines, as well as for cooking and heating. Put them on your check list to do before you set sail. It is surprising how often fuel and water get forgotten. Fresh water tanks need flushing through regularly if they are to stay fresh. A spare can of fresh water should always be carried for emergency use and this also needs changing as often as possible. It is part of your safety kit.

Safety

This subject has had its own chapter, but a check list included in your planning should make sure you do not miss anything. Do not forget things like spare clothing, and waterproofs for *everyone*.

CG 66 system

Letting someone ashore know where you are going and when you expect to arrive comes in this section. Let the Coastguard know when you are leaving and, if it is your boat, use the CG 66 system. This is a system whereby you fill in a little card with a full description of your boat and the name and address of a contact ashore. This card is lodged with your local coastguard rescue centre. If you do get into difficulties, the card provides valuable information for any rescue attempt. You should notify the person named on the card when you leave and when you expect to arrive at your destination (or its alternative). In this way, failure to arrive will be noticed and also false alarms can be avoided. Do not forget to let them know when you *do* arrive.

The reason for it all

You will have noticed, I am sure, that in this chapter are included various headings that have chapters of their own earlier in the book. This is really what it is all about; putting together all that you know, so that you can plan, and make, successful passages.

At first your passages will be small and short. However short, each will seem like an adventure to you. This is how it should be. Gradually, as you gain in both experience and in confidence, you will extend your horizons and venture much further afield.

When you do, I hope you will feel that *The Shorebased Sailor* has helped you to start from a solid foundation! Learning to sail involves learning a good deal of theory, principles, methods etc. Sailing itself, if it is to be enjoyable and satisfying, involves a great deal of planning and preparation.

If you decide to take part in the RYA Cruising Scheme and start to take the various courses available, you will find that the knowledge gained from this book will help you at all levels. If you intend to go it alone, you have a sound basis from which to build. Either way, sailing a cruiser is a great experience, to be enjoyed all the more if you feel confident that you know what you are doing.

Glossary

————————— ⚓ —————————

ABAFT   When something is seen in a direction that is behind the beam relative to the direction in which a vessel is heading, it is said to be 'abaft the beam'.

ADMIRALTY CHART   A chart produced and published by the Hydrographer to the Navy.

AFT   Towards the back of a vessel as in 'looking aft' or actually at the back as in 'the cockpit is aft'.

AIMING OFF   To deliberately head for a point to one side of one's objective.

ALMANAC   A book containing data that changes annually. A nautical almanac contains essentially, tidal and astronomical data relating to the sea.

ARC OF VISIBILITY   The segment of a circle round a light between two radii, in which the light is visible.

ASTERN   In a direction directly behind a vessel.

BEACON   Originally a signal fire but now a tower, post or similar object driven into the sea bed or on the shore for use as a navigation mark.

BILGE   The lowest point in a boat into which water drains.

BINNACLE   The pedestal and housing used to mount a steering compass to protect it from the weather.

BOLLARD   A wooden or metal post to which mooring lines are attached. Often found in pairs.

BOLT CROPPERS   A heavy duty pair of cutters operated by hand and capable of sheering through bolts or steel cables.

BOWLINE   A knot used to form a temporary loop in the end of a rope.

BRITISH SUMMER TIME   A method used to delay sunset in summer by adding an hour to true, or Greenwich Mean Time.

BRUCE   A type of anchor cast from solid metal and having no moving parts.

BUNG   A plug of material, usually soft wood or rubber, used to close a hole to prevent the passage of liquids.

BUNK BOARD   Loose wooden cover to a storage under a berth.

BUOY   A floating anchored object used as a mark at sea. Usually distinguished by colour and shape.

BUTANE A heavy carbon based gas which can be liquefied under pressure and is used as a fuel.

CQR An anchor shaped like a plough. The letters stand for Chatham Quick Release.

CAPSIZE To turn over so that the side normally down is uppermost.

CARDINAL MARKS A system of buoyage based on the cardinal or main points of the compass.

CATENARY The natural curve taken by a rope or chain when supported only at its ends.

CHAFE To wear away as a result of friction.

CLEARING LINE A bearing or direction to steer indicating the boundary between safe water and water containing possible hazards.

CLEAT A solid fitting having two horns or projections around which a rope may be made fast.

CLEVIS PIN A smooth cylindrical pin, flanged at one end, used to close a shackle. It is secured by a split pin or ring passing through it.

CLOSING SITUATION The situation that exists when two vessels are approaching each other.

CLOVE HITCH A type of knot or (correctly) bend used to secure a rope to a fixed object.

COCKED HAT The triangle formed when three position lines fail to cross at a point.

COCKPIT The sunken area in a sailing vessel in which the helmsman sits.

COLLISION REGULATIONS Popular name for the International Regulations for the Prevention of Collisions at Sea.

COMPASS ADJUSTER A professional who checks and corrects marine compasses in situ.

COMPOSITE FIX A fix in which the position lines have been obtained by more than one method.

CONSTRUCTION A geometrical method of calculation using diagrams.

CORRECTED CHART A chart on which information available subsequent to its production has been entered.

COURSE CHANGE An alteration in the direction in which a vessel is steered.

COURSE AND DISTANCE MADE GOOD See 'ground track'.

CROWN Part of an anchor at which the arms meet the shank.

DAMPING of a compass. The means whereby a compass card is prevented from moving freely in response to sudden movements of the instrument, or the observed effect of this reduced movement.

DAN BUOY A small temporary buoy used for emergency marking. Normally fitted with an extension shaft carrying a flag.

DANFORTH An American design of anchor which can be stowed flat. It is common on large vessels.

DEAD RECKONING A means of establishing one's position using measured distance and direction only.

DEPARTURE POINT　The actual position from which a passage starts and from which all navigational plotting originates.

DEVIATION　The error in a compass reading as a result of proximity of ferrous or conducting materials within its field.

DIPPING DISTANCE　The distance between the observer and a light at which the light dips below the horizon.

DOUGLAS PROTRACTOR　see 'Portland protractor'.

DRIFT　Any movement of an object relative to land resulting only from movement of the water carrying it or the movement of the water.

EBB　The period of a tide when the water level is falling.

ECHO SOUNDER　A device for measuring the depth of water by means of detecting the echo of an ultrasonic signal off the sea bed.

EDGE-READ　A means of reading a compass from a scale printed on the edge rather than the top of the card.

ESTIMATED POSITION　A position found by applying correction for tide and leeway to a dead reckoning position.

ESTUARY　The water at the mouth of a river where it meets the sea.

FAIRLEAD　A solid smooth fitting used to direct a rope or line so as to avoid chafe.

FENDER　Soft, usually air filled, cushion used to protect the side of a vessel when lying alongside.

FIGURE-OF-EIGHT　A knot used to form a stop in the end of a rope.

FIX　A position found using bearings from fixed objects.

FLOOD　The period of a tide when the water level is rising.

FORESTAY　A mast support connected to the fore part of the vessel.

FOUL　As in 'foul ground'. A sea bed on which material is likely to catch or 'foul' an anchor, e.g. old chain, weeds etc.

GNOMONIC PROJECTION　A method of chart production in which the global sphere is in point contact only with the plane of the chart.

GROUND TRACK　The path actually travelled over the ground by a moving vessel.

GYBE　A manoeuvre in which a vessel is turned across the wind in such a way that the wind changes sides from astern.

HALLIARD　A line used to hoist a sail.

HEAD-TO-TAIL　To join end to end so that all parts point in the same direction.

HEAVING LINE　A light line weighted at one end, used for throwing in order to pass a heavier line attached to it.

HELMSMAN　The individual actually steering a vessel.

HOIST　To raise into the air as 'hoist the sails'.

HOLDING GROUND　The bottom into which the anchor digs in order to hold a vessel.

HYDROGRAPHER　A maker of marine maps.

IALA   The abbreviation, said as one word, for the International Association of Light Authorities.

IN-HULL LOG   Instrument used to measure speed by means of a sensor projecting through the hull of the vessel.

ISOPHASE   A light, having equal periods of light and darkness.

JACK STAYS   Lines running parallel to the deck of a vessel to provide attachments for safety lines.

KEDGE   Originally to refloat a vessel aground by pulling off. Now normally used to refer to an anchor used over the stern of the vessel, or as a back-up anchor.

LAID (rope)   A rope in which the fibres are set parallel and twisted together in bunches, normally three, called lays.

LANYARD   A light line used as a fastening.

LATERAL MARKS   Buoys placed on either side of a channel to mark its confines.

LATITUDE   A method of indicating a position north or south of the equator by a series of concentric circles starting at the equator. The circle positions are fixed by the angle subtended between them and the equator at the centre of the earth.

LEADING LINE   A line or bearing which if followed will lead a vessel on a safe track clear of all dangers.

LEEWAY   The sideways movement of a vessel, away from its heading, over the water as a result of a lateral force from the wind.

LOG   The instrument used to measure a vessel's speed through the water. Also the document recording the conduct of a vessel on passage.

LONGITUDE   A system of locating a position circumferentially on the earth by dividing the surface into 360 segments expressed in degrees away from an arbitrary position line passing through Greenwich. Each segment bisects both geostatic poles.

LOOM   Reflection seen in the sky, of a light a little below the horizon.

MAGNETIC BEARING   A bearing produced by a compass as a result of the earth's magnetic field.

MAGNETIC COMPASS   A compass using a magnetised needle as a sensing device.

MAGNETIC POLES   The notional positions of the poles of the earth's magnetic field. They are close to, but not coincident with, the geographical poles.

MARLIN SPIKE   Originally 'marling'. A pointed object used in splicing rope to separate the lays.

MAYDAY   From the French *m'aidez* meaning 'help me'. It is the international radio-telephone distress signal.

MEAN   Average.

MERCATOR PROJECTION   A means of chart production in which the global sphere is coincident with the plane of the chart about its equator.

MOORING LINE   A line used to secure a vessel to the shore or to some fixed object attached to the shore.

NAUTICAL ALMANAC   see 'almanac'.

NAUTICAL MILE   The mean value of one minute of arc of one degree of latitude. Now accepted as a distance of 1853 metres which is approximately 1.1 land miles.

NAVIGATION LIGHTS   Those lights required to be shown by a vessel at night to indicate both motion and the direction of that motion.

NEAP TIDE   A tide within the tide cycle in which the range is minimal for that cycle. It occurs when the sun and moon are at right angles in relation to the earth.

OCCULTING   A light which flashes with the periods of darkness being shorter than the periods of light.

OSCILLATION   A cyclical movement about a mean point as between successive wave crests and troughs.

OVERFALLS   An area of disturbed water resulting from the movement of the tide over a raised area on the sea bed.

PARACHUTE ROCKET   An illuminating signal flare projected into the air by rocket power having a parachute to slow its descent.

PERIOD   The time interval between successive cycles of events. In light signals the time taken between the start of its light pattern until it starts to repeat the pattern.

PILOT BOOK   A book giving details of navigational hazards and local conditions relating to specific areas or harbours.

PILOTAGE   The art of navigating a vessel based on the recognition of local signs and conditions.

PLOTTING   The drawing of geometrical constructions on a chart in order to ascertain one's position.

PORT   A harbour generally used by large vessels for commercial purposes, *or* the left side of a vessel, or in that direction, when facing towards the front.

PORT TACK   A sailing vessel having the wind blowing from the port side is said to be on port tack. More specifically the vessel is on port tack when the main fore-and-aft sail is carried on the starboard side.

PORTLAND PROTRACTOR   A patent navigational protractor having square sides set parallel and at right angles to the North/South index.

POSITION LINE   A line drawn on a chart, based on the bearing of an object, on which the vessel must be positioned.

PRISM   A triangular glass cylinder having the ability to refract light so that it is turned through a right angle.

PROPANE   A heavy carbon based gas which can be liquefied under pressure. Used as a heating fuel.

PYROTECHNICS   The group name for signals commonly called flares.

QUADRANT A quarter of a circle, *or* one of a group of instruments based on the quadrant.

QUARTERS The back corners of a vessel or in that direction, on or from, the vessel.

RADAR REFLECTOR A metal device capable of returning signals transmitted by radar along a parallel path, thus increasing the strength of signal at the detecting apparatus.

RADIO LOG A documentary record of all messages transmitted and received by radio. Required to be kept by anyone operating a radio transmitter under licence.

REEF To reduce the area of a sail by tying a part of it away out of the wind, or that part of the sail tied up, *or* the knot used for tying reefs.

RELATIVE MOTION When one object is moving in relation to another which is itself also moving, the change of position between the two objects is called their relative motion.

RESULTANT When two or more vectors are combined the cumulative effect of them all is the resultant.

RHUMB LINE A line joining two places on a chart, representing the shortest distance between them.

ROLLING HITCH A hitch used to attach one line to another under tension.

RULE OF TWELFTHS A simplified method of calculating tide heights based on the sine wave. The range is divided into 12 parts and it is assumed that the height will change by 1, 2 and 3 parts successively in each of the first 3 hours and by 3, 2 and 1 part in the last 3 hours.

RUNNING FIX A method of position fixing by using successive position lines obtained from the same object.

SCOPE The amount of cable between a set anchor and its attachment point on the vessel.

SEA STATE The condition of the sea surface resulting from wind and tide.

SEA MARKS Marks used for position finding which float on the sea, as opposed to land marks.

SECONDARY PORT A port for which no detailed tidal information is recorded. Such detail has to be derived from data for a standard port.

SECTORED A light which does not show over a complete circle is said to be sectored. The circle may be divided into sectors of light and dark, or of different colours.

SET To put in position as in 'set the sails', *or* the direction of a tidal stream.

SEIZE To bind with wire a shackle pin, or with light line the free end of a rope, in a knot to the standing part. In each case the object is to prevent accidental release of the fastening.

SHACKLE A bow or 'D' shaped piece of metal closed with a pin and used to join chain or rope to a chain or boat fitting.

SHIP'S HEADING The direction in which a vessel is pointing.

SHIP'S LOG   A documentary record of the conduct of a vessel at sea.

SMALL CRAFT EDITION   As in 'M' notices. A special edition of the chart, correcting information containing only that information likely to be of interest to small vessels.

SNATCH LOAD   A load which is applied suddenly rather than progressively.

SOUNDING   The measured depth of water above the sea bed.

SPINNAKER   Large balloon sail flown loose luffed forward of all other sails.

SPLICE   The joining of two ropes by weaving strands of one rope between those of the other or the forming of a loop in a rope by the same means.

SPRING TIDE   A tide in which the range is at the maximum in that cycle. It occurs when the sun and moon are in line with the earth.

STANDARD PORT   One of the reference ports for which full tidal data is available.

STANDING PART   That part of a secured rope which is in tension.

STARBOARD   The side of a vessel which is on one's right when facing forward, or in that direction as, 'to starboard'.

STOPPER KNOT   Any knot tied in a rope to prevent the end running through a block, fairlead or eye when it is released.

STREAM   The horizontal movement of water as a result of tidal effects.

STROP   A normally short length of rope or webbing used as a restraint.

SWINGING CIRCLE   The circle described by a moored vessel as a result of its moving with the tide's ebb and flow.

TACK   The lower leading corner of a sail.

TACK (TO)   To move a vessel so that the direction of the wind changes from one side to the other.

TAKE A BEARING   The act of using a compass to measure the bearing to any object.

THIMBLE   A circular or pear-shaped hard fitting used to reinforce a loop in a rope or cable.

THREE POINT FIX   A position found by using three position lines.

TIDAL ATLAS   A book of chartlets showing the tidal stream and set for each hour over a 12 hour period.

TIDAL DIAMOND   A chart symbol used to locate the position at which tidal data, tabulated on the chart, was measured.

TIDAL VECTOR   A line drawn on a chart to represent the magnitude and direction of tide over a period.

TIDE SET   See 'set'.

TRAILING LOG   An instrument used to measure rate of movement through the water by means of a sensing device towed behind the vessel.

TRANSIT LINE   A straight line joining two fixed points, the extension of which will produce a position line. A vessel seeing the two points in line is said to be 'on transit'.

TRIPPING LINE   A line attached to the crown of an anchor before it is lowered in order to enable the anchor to be freed if it becomes fouled.

TRUE BEARING   A bearing in relation to the geographical poles.

VARIATION   The difference between a true and a magnetic bearing due to the changing position of the magnetic poles.

VECTOR   A mathematical term for a line which represents both magnitude and direction.

VEER (TO)   A change in the wind direction in a clockwise direction, *or* the act of letting out anchor cable, *or* the sideways movement of a vessel when at anchor.

WAKE   The track of disturbed water left by the passage of a vessel.

WAKE COURSE   The direction of the line of the wake of a vessel.

WATER TRACK   The path traced by a vessel over the surface of the water.

WHIPPING   The binding of a rope end with thin line to prevent it from unravelling or fraying.

WIND STRENGTH   The velocity of the wind. It may be given in terms of metres per second, miles per hour or in terms of the Beaufort wind scale.

WINDWARD   Towards the direction from which the wind is blowing.

YACHT   A vessel used for pleasure purposes, generally relating to one powered by sails but not specifically so.

Appendix A

— ⚓ —

Exercises and answers

Chapter 1

Answers to names of boat parts required in Figure 1.1

A	Mast Head
B	Forestay
C	Fore (or Jib) Halliard
D	Leach (of Mainsail)
E	Head (of Jib)
F	Spreader
G	Batten Pocket
H	Mast
I	Shroud
J	Jib
K	Luff (of Jib)
L	Boom
M	Backstay
N	Jib Sheet
O	Kicking Strap
P	Main Sheet
Q	Pulpit
R	Pushpit
S	Stem
T	Stanchions
U	Sheet Winch
V	Tiller
W	Keel
X	Rudder

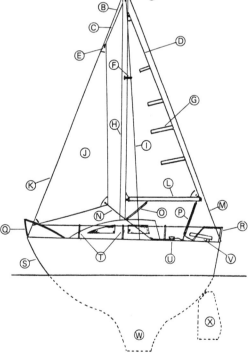

Fig. A.1 Parts of a boat (Repeat of Fig 1.1)

Chapter 5

Fig. A.2 Example 5.1: Which stands on, and why?

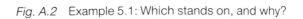

Fig. A.3 Example 5.2: Which stands on, and why?

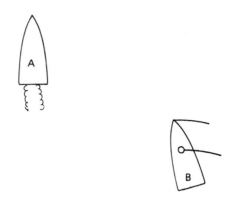

Fig. A.4 Example 5.3: Which stands on, and why?

Fig. A.5 Example 5.4: Which stands on, and why?

Answers

Example 5.1 'B' stands on
  Both vessels on the same tack (port)
  Windward boat keeps clear
Example 5.2 'A' stands on
  Both vessels under power
  Vessel with the other on its starboard gives way
Example 5.3 'A' stands on
  Overtaking vessel keeps clear even when under sail overtaking a vessel under power
Example 5.4 'B' stands on
  Under sail on opposite tacks
  Vessel on port tack gives way to vessel on starboard

Chapter 6

Exercises on using a Portland protractor (use copy chart shown, page 108)

Notes: 1 The actual location of a charted mark is at the small circle at the base of the symbol.
  2 Assume variation if required is 6 degrees West.
  3 The symbols required are shown in Figure 6.1.
  4 Shipping lanes are indicated by outlined arrow shapes.

Question 1 What is the true bearing from Varne light-vessel to South Goodwin light-vessel?
Question 2 In what direction would you steer to go up the channel following the North East bound shipping lane?
Question 3 What is the bearing from Sandettie light-vessel to West Dyck port hand buoy?

Answers

Question 1 024 degrees (true)
Question 2 048 degrees (magnetic)
Question 3 159 degrees (true)

Chapter 7

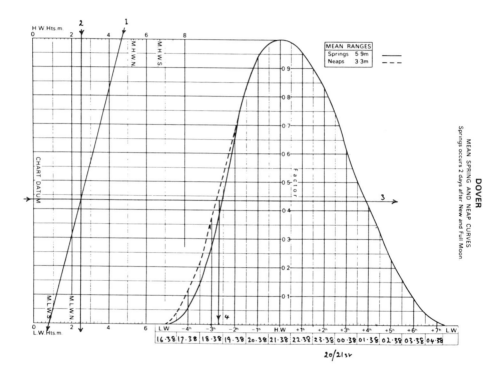

Fig. A.6   Fig. 7.5 (completed)

Example 7.1

1   It is the 12th August 1986 and you are in Ramsgate Marina. You are
    intending to sail that day on a cruise. You do not expect your crew to
    arrive until mid-day. How late after mid-day could you leave?
2   Use the information from Figures 7.2 and 7.3 and the Dover tidal curve
    shown to find your clearance over the bottom in the dredged (2.1 metre)
    channel at your departure time if your boat draws 1.8 metres.

Answers to Example 7.1

1	Tides	Dover	Time	Height	Ramsgate	Time	Height
	12th Aug HW		15.08	6.1m	HW	15.28	4.4m
	LW		09.52	1.5m	LW	09.45	0.9m

Gates open Ramsgate Marina HW −2 hours to HW +1 hour
Latest departure time: **16.28 i.e. HW +1 hour (or 17.28 BST)**

2 Depth at HW +1 = 4.3m + 2.1 (drying height) − 1.8 (draught) = **4.6m**
See diagram for tidal curve plotting

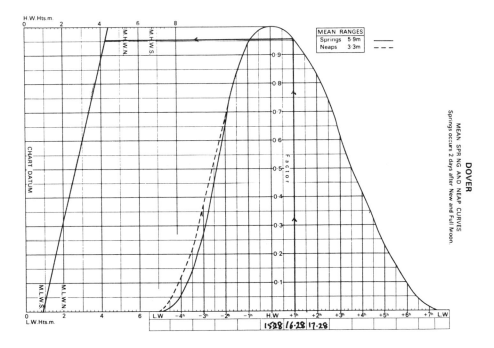

Fig. A.7 Example 7.1: Worked answer

Example 7.2

1 In the same yacht on 6th May you were at Dover in the inner harbour.
What would be the earliest time you could have left, with a 1.0 metre
safety margin, if the entrance dries 2.1 metres at chart datum?
Use the data and tidal curve as in Example 7.1.

Answer to Example 7.2

1   Tides   Dover   Time   Height
    6th May   HW   09.42   6.0m
                  LW   04.47   0.9m
    Rise   2.1 (drying height) + 1.8 (draught) + 1.0 (safety)
    required: = 4.9m. **This will occur at 08.00**
    See diagram for tidal curve plotting

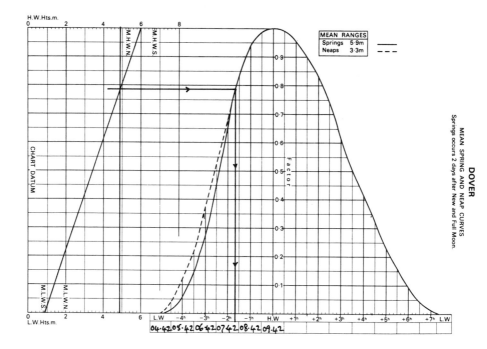

Fig. A.8   Example 7.2: Worked answer

Chapter 8

Answers to Examples 8.1 and 8.2 are shown on the graph. The distances you should have obtained were:

   Example 8.1 – **15.5 miles (approx)**
   Example 8.2 – **28.6 miles (approx)**

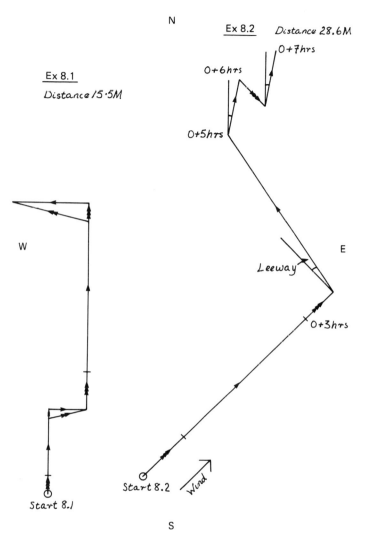

N

Ex 8.2   *Distance 28.6M*

0+7hrs

0+6hrs

Ex 8.1

Distance 15·5M

0+5hrs

W   E

Leeway

0+3hrs

Start 8.2   *Wind*

Start 8.1

S

Fig. A.9 Examples 8.1 and 8.2: Answers

Appendix B

───────────── ⚓ ─────────────

This appendix is divided into three sections. Each section covers a part of the boat. To use it, find the section relating to the area you are studying and work through each paragraph. Each jargon word or term is put into a sentence in such a way that its meaning should be clear. If it is not, refer to the Glossary.

The hull from outside

The whole body of the boat, the solid bit, is the hull. When it floats the bit above meets the bit below at the WATER LINE. The distance from the front, or sharp end, called the BOW to the blunter back end, the STERN, at this level, is the WATER LINE LENGTH usually written LWL, whilst the greatest length from bow to stern is called the LENGTH OVERALL, written LOA.

The greatest width is called the BEAM and the depth from the water line to the lowest point is the DRAUGHT. The bit that sticks down at about the middle is the KEEL which usually contains a lot of dead weight to stop the boat tipping over too much; this is called BALLAST. At the back is the RUDDER, which is turned in the water to steer the boat, by the TILLER. This is a crank lever fitted to the top of the TILLER POST which comes up, either into the COCKPIT, or immediately behind it. The cockpit is a depression at the back of the deck in which the crew can sit.

The sharp edge at the front leading up to the bow is the STEM whilst the blunt bit across the stern is the TRANSOM. The DECK is the lid that covers the top of the hull. If it has a raised bit as in Figure 1.1, this is called the COACH HOUSE. Any windows in this are LIGHTS, and the MAST, which rises up to support the sails, can be either DECK STEPPED or KEEL STEPPED depending on whether it is mounted on a STEP fitted on the top of the deck, or goes through the deck and down to the keel.

Round, and over, the bow is fitted a rigid metal frame, called the PULPIT. This has wires, GUARD RAILS, running AFT, through supporting pillars called STANCHIONS to the back, where the rails are connected to a similar frame called the PUSHPIT which fits on the top of the transom.

The mast is kept upright by at least four wires, together called STANDING RIGGING. The one connected to the bow is the FORESTAY, the one to the stern, the BACKSTAY and the ones to the sides of the boat are SHROUDS. These are often held away from the mast somewhere near the top by SPREADERS. The shrouds are connected to the hull by means of CHAIN PLATES. They may be attached to the chain plates by screw tensioning devices called BOTTLE SCREWS. The forestay is attached to the STEMHEAD FITTING at the top of the stem, which may also carry the ANCHOR ROLLER.

The last seven paragraphs have put names to quite a number of items all of which are useful to know. All the things I have named so far stay where they are when the boat is in use, except the steering gear. In the next section the bits that move about when sailing are named. Most of these you *must* know as crew because you will be told to, 'pull the sheet in! Tighten the main halliard! Mind the boom!' and so on, and so on.

Sails, mast and control system

The RIGGING covers all the wires and ropes that hold up the mast and support the sails. Standing rigging is so called because it keeps the mast standing up. The sails are raised, controlled and lowered on RUNNING RIGGING. The HALLIARDS are the ropes or wires used to hoist and lower all sails and a specific name identifies the sail to which a particular one is attached. Thus the MAIN halliard controls the MAINSAIL.

The MAINSAIL is the sail which runs directly up the MAINMAST, or the largest mast, if the boat has more than one. Its lower edge is attached to a rigid pole or BOOM which is fitted at right angles to the mast by means of a swivel fitting called the GOOSENECK. The mainsail is connected to both mast and boom, called SPARS, either by sliding the edge of the sail, which is thickened with a BOLT ROPE into a groove, or by means of slides attached to the sail which run in a track.

Each sail has three corners. The top one is the HEAD, the bottom one at the front is the TACK and that at the back is the CLEW.

In times gone by the tack of the sail was actually nailed to a spar with brass tacks. Could this be the origin of the expression 'getting down to brass tacks'? They would certainly be essentials. The term 'clew' gives us another cliché. 'I haven't got a clew!' called down from the yard arm by the lad sent aloft to 'bend on' the rope to the corner of a huge square sail as it billowed in the wind, would indicate that he had not got the right idea of how to do the job.

The three edges also have names. The edge that joins the head to the tack and meets the wind first is the LUFF. The edge between the head and the clew, off which the wind flows, is the LEACH. This edge, on the mainsail, is usually stiffened by lathes of wood or composition called BATTENS fitted in BATTEN POCKETS. The bottom edge of the sail is the FOOT. On the mainsail the foot is tightened by a line, called the OUTHAUL, connected from the clew to the outer end of the boom.

The boom is prevented from falling down when no sail is on it by the TOPPING LIFT, a rope which runs from the end of the boom to the top of the mast where it is fed over a pulley or SHEAVE in a SHEAVE BLOCK and back down to the deck so that it can be adjusted. Halliards also run through sheave blocks in the mast. To stop the boom kicking up when the wind catches the sail a device called a KICKING STRAP is connected from the foot of the mast to a point on the boom about one fifth of the way from the gooseneck. The kicking strap may consist of a block and tackle arrangement or it may be a piston in a sleeve whose movement is controlled by gas or oil.

Apart from the mainsail, a yacht will have HEADSAILS or FORESAILS which are fitted in the front of the boat onto the forestay by means of either spring loaded clips attached to the luff called PISTON HANKS or it may, like the mainsail, have a bolt rope which runs up a LUFF GROOVE. The latter will always be so if the yacht is fitted with a FURLING GEAR so that part or all of the sail can be rolled round the forestay.

The foresails have names which depend on their size. Any which has an area greater than the FORE TRIANGLE, which is the triangle formed by the forestay, mast and deck, is called a GENOA. A foresail which is smaller than the fore triangle is a JIB. The foresails are numbered from the largest down, so if the yacht has three genoas, the largest will be number 1 and the smallest number 3. The very smallest jib is usually extra strongly made and, instead of being given a number, may simply be called the STORM JIB,

The big, often coloured, balloon shaped sail that attracts the eye on a warm day with a light wind is a SPINNAKER. This sail has its own boom, halliard and several other control lines not needed for other headsails. The names of these are best learned in practice.

If the yacht has a second, smaller mast it is a MIZZEN mast and its equivalent to the mainsail is the MIZZEN SAIL. If set on stays, they are MIZZEN STAYSAILS.

All sails are controlled by ropes, called SHEETS, which are attached to the clew. This is done directly in the case of the foresails and staysails, but on the mainsail the sheet is connected, through SHEET BLOCKS to the end of the boom and to the deck. This is because the force on the mainsail is more easily controlled using a pulley system. The lower end of the MAINSHEET pulley system is usually connected to the deck, in the cockpit area via a device called a TRAVELLER so that it can be hauled across from side to side to suit sailing conditions.

The sheets for the foresail (there are usually two with one led along each side of the boat to the cockpit) often run through adjustable sliding blocks on rails or SHEET TRACKS. This is so that the angle of pull on them can be adjusted before they are led onto SHEET WINCHES which are used to take the strain when adjusting sheet tension. Winches are geared drums. A rope wound round a few turns can be winched in and a great deal of tension can be applied without much effort.

Sometimes the direction at which the sheet comes onto the winch needs to be adjusted. This is done by taking the sheet through a small block mounted in the appropriate place. Any device for directing a rope in the best direction without rubbing is called a FAIRLEAD. The open topped oval slots through which MOORING LINES are led when attaching the boat to the shore are examples of fairleads.

Ropes, once correctly positioned, are normally fastened by securing to a CLEAT. This is a rigid shape in metal, wood or plastic, having two horns around which the rope is twisted. Some have a tapered slot on one side so that they are self JAMMING, others use a pair of claws to do the same thing.

Inside the yacht

To get inside one usually goes through a HATCHWAY from the cockpit. This hatch is normally closed vertically with removable panels called WASHBOARDS. The top of the hatch is normally closed by means of a sliding HATCH COVER. The stairs that lead down into the main CABIN or SALOON are the COMPANIONWAY. The floor of the cabin is the CABIN SOLE and the ceiling, the DECKHEAD. Various furnishings will be found in the saloon. Any cupboards are called LOCKERS and the kitchen area is the GALLEY. Any beds are BERTHS. Walls between areas are BULKHEADS. A bulkhead normally separates the toilet area or HEADS and the FORECABIN which is the sleeping area at the front. Some yachts will have an AFTERCABIN or cabins at the back whilst others simply have QUARTER BERTHS running under the cockpit.

Any holes in the hull for the intake or outlet of fluids will, if they are below the water line, be closed by SEA COCKS. The lowest point in the hull, into which any water will drain, is the BILGE which can be cleared with the BILGE PUMP. Fresh water is often stored in tanks under the berths. Access to these under berth lockers or BINS is usually by means of lift out panels called BUNK BOARDS. Fixed to the sides of the bunks will be LEE CLOTHS or sometimes LEE BOARDS which prevent one falling out of the berth when the boat heels over.

Appendix C

_____ ⚓ _____

Use of VHF in Distress Situations

Mayday

This is the international code word for distress. It must only be used _when the vessel is in imminent danger._

Two points to note here:

1 It is the vessel not individual crew members that must be in danger.
2 The danger must be imminent. Mayday is not to be used when the danger is possible, or even probable, at some future time.

Mayday procedure

1 _Call_: 'MAYDAY MAYDAY MAYDAY – this is Firebrand Firebrand Firebrand – MAYDAY Firebrand – three miles south west of Needles[1] – am on fire and sinking[2] – require lifeboat or helicopter[3] – abandoning to liferaft – four adults – one with serious burns – have channel 16 in raft – OVER.'
2 Listen for reply for one minute. If nothing heard, repeat call.
3 _If you hear a call_: First listen to see if a ship or shore station who will be better equipped to deal with it answers. If nothing heard you _must either_ answer _or_ re-transmit the call as a MAYDAY RELAY.
4 _Relay Call_: 'MAYDAY RELAY MAYDAY RELAY MAYDAY RELAY – this is Flame Flame Flame – MAYDAY Firebrand – three miles south . . . (repeat _exact_ words of original call) – OVER.'

Notes

1 It is essential that your position is given immediately after your identity in case that is all you have time for! Always give your position _from_ a fixed reference point if possible. A latitude and longitude position is more

prone to error, takes more time to put out and to receive and is slower for rescuers to locate.

2 The nature of distress is helpful in rescue work.
3 Say what help you need.
   Only then should you give other information of use to your would-be rescuers and *make this brief.*

If you hear MAYDAY write down everything you hear. You may *only hear it once* and you may be the *only person to hear it.*

Index